ANTIQUITIES OF THE
IRISH COUNTRYSIDE

Antiquities
of the Irish Countryside

by
SEÁN P. Ó RÍORDÁIN

METHUEN & CO LTD
11 NEW FETTER LANE EC4

First Published 1942
Second edition 1943
First Published by Methuen & Co Ltd
(Third edition revised & reset) 1953
Fourth edition 1965
Reprinted 1966
Reprinted 1968
S.B.N. 416 54610 2

4.3

First Published as a University Paperback 1965
Reprinted 1966
Reprinted 1968
S.B.N. 416 68440 8

1.3

Printed in Great Britain by
Fletcher & Son Ltd, Norwich

Distributed in the U.S.A.
by Barnes & Noble Inc.

CONTENTS

TEXT ILLUSTRATIONS

PLATES

71. V-shaped passage-grave, Carriglong, Co. Waterford. (*Courtesy: Cork Historical and Archaeological Society. Photo: T. G. E. Powell*)

72. Stone alignment, 'Finn Mac Cool's Fingers', Shantemon, Co. Cavan. (*Photo: Author*)

73. Megalithic cist from Chapelizod, Co. Dublin (now in Zoological Gardens, Dublin). (*Photo: Rev. C. Scantlebury*)

74. Cist burial, Keenoge, Co. Meath, showing skeleton and Food Vessel. (*Photo: National Museum of Ireland*)

75. Long cist grave at Cush, Co. Limerick—broken Food Vessel in position. (*Courtesy: Royal Irish Academy. Photo: Author*)

76. Short cist grave at Cush—urn in position. (*Courtesy: Royal Irish Academy. Photo: Author*)

77. 'Mound of the Hostages', Tara, Co. Meath. (*Photo: Author*)

78. Barrow at Rathjordan, Co. Limerick. (*Photo: Author*)

79. Tumulus at Lattin, Co. Tipperary. (*Photo: Author*)

80. Tumulus at Cush, Co. Limerick—during excavation, showing fosse. (*Courtesy: Royal Irish Academy. Photo: Author*)

81. Standing stone, Punchestown, Co. Kildare. (*Photo: H. S. Crawford*)

82. Ogham stone, Minard, Co. Kerry. (*Photo: C. Ó Danachair*)

83. Stone with Iron Age ornament, Turoe, Co. Galway. (*Courtesy: Royal Society of Antiquaries of Ireland. Photo: J. Raftery*)

84. Inscribed standing stone, Ballyvourney, Co. Cork. (*Photo: M. J. O'Kelly*)

85. Cross-inscribed ogham stone, Dromkeare, Co. Kerry. (*Photo: C. Ó Danachair*)

86. Stone circles, Grange, Lough Gur, Co. Limerick. (*Photo: Aerofilms*)

87. Stone circle, Drombeg, Co. Cork. (*Photo: Fógra Fáilte*)

88. Lisivigeen stone circle, Killarney, Co. Kerry. (*Photo: Author*)

PREFACE TO FIRST EDITION

This booklet is not intended for specialists in archaeology. Its purpose is to give some answer to the questioning man in the street, who asks the archaeologist for a simple explanation of some monument which he has noticed in the countryside and which is, in all probability, a typical example of a class of antiquity widespread throughout Ireland.

The question usually concerns an individual structure, be it fort, souterrain, stone circle, or other antiquity, of which the archaeologist, lacking evidence which excavation might yield, can say little. He can, however, explain at some length what is known of this *type* of monument. So that such information may be available in a convenient printed form it is proposed to give an outline here of the present state of knowledge concerning those classes of antiquities most frequently met with in the Irish countryside, and it is hoped that our brief notes will make them intelligible to the inquiring layman. Monuments, (churches, high crosses, round towers, and so on) belonging specifically to Early Christianity are not dealt with here, since their study involves the subjects of architecture and art rather than archaeology proper, and it is proposed to confine our survey to the types of monuments most common throughout the country.

It would serve no useful purpose to burden the reader with questions of chronology, but some rough idea of dates is necessary that the few simple technical terms used may be understood. Prehistoric time is divided into three main periods —the Stone, Bronze, and Early Iron Ages. The earliest period, the Stone Age, is subdivided into the Early, Middle, and Late Stone Ages—only the last of which need concern us here. This Late Stone Age, or Neolithic period must, in Ireland, be regarded as a very brief one covering perhaps a century or two before and after 2000 B.C. and inextricably overlapping with the incoming Bronze Age. The Bronze Age may be taken as extending from about 2000 B.C. to 500 B.C. and is conveniently subdivided into Early, Middle, and Late phases, each of 500 years duration. Mention will be made here of the Beaker Folk.

These are a people known from their distinctive type of pottery (Beakers), who arrived in Great Britain and, as excavation has recently demonstrated, in Ireland also, during the Early Bronze Age. The Early Iron Age is regarded as the period from about 500 B.C. to the fifth century A.D. when Christianity was introduced. The succeeding centuries are spoken of as the Early Christian period which is followed (from the eleventh century) by Medieval times; (the term 'Medieval' is used here in its more restricted sense, and covers the later Middle Ages only as distinct from the 'Early Christian' centuries).

Scarcely any of the chronological points in this brief summary would fail to give rise, among archaeologists, to violent discussion, and should, in any more technical publication, be hedged round with qualifying statements. They may, however, be taken, in broad outline, as a useful time scale, provided the reader remembers that the periods are not sharply divided one from another but, rather, that considerable overlap occurs and that implements and monuments found already in Neolithic contexts may, in some cases, be also at home in Early Iron Age, or even later times.

Since this booklet is for the general reader, who may have no ambitions or opportunity to delve deeply into the voluminous archaeological literature which might be invoked on each of the topics covered, it is not intended to encumber the text pages with references. Should the reader wish more fully to acquaint himself with the subject, the Bibliography at the end may be found useful. With the aid of this, he should be in a position to evaluate for himself the evidence produced by excavation and by field surveys.

It is the hope of the writer that, having read the pages that follow, the reader may be stimulated to seek for himself examples of the antiquities therein described. Should he wish to do so, he is strongly advised to procure for himself a copy of the 6-inch Ordnance Sheet covering the district in which he is interested. These maps are invaluable and must serve as the basis for any proposed Field Survey. While on some sheets the sites of almost all monuments are recorded, on others the omissions will be found to be numerous, this being particularly true of mountainous areas. The enthusiast with a flair for field-work can do immense service to archaeology by undertaking an accurate survey of all the ancient remains in some one district. Such a survey calls for detailed plans and descriptions of all sites, whether recorded by the O.S. or not. Its careful compilation will, in many instances, bring to notice monuments unknown to Irish Archaeology, while it should, in any case, serve to make more complete our still very inadequate knowledge of field antiquities particularly in the matter of the distribution of the different types.

(*Note added in Third Edition:*

The date 500 B.C. is retained in the above chronological scheme. It appears to mark conveniently a point at which Iron Age influences are felt, but it must be admitted that at present there is little evidence for a real Iron Age in Ireland until the first century B.C.)

PREFACE TO THIRD EDITION

Antiquities of the Irish Countryside was first published in 1942 by the Cork University Press; a second edition (which embodied minor changes only) was published in 1943 but it has been out of print for some time. Its re-publication has been delayed by the fact that subsequent research, new discoveries, and further excavations made it necessary to re-write large portions. The present edition (in an altered format) is published with the kind consent of the Cork University Press and in it an attempt is made to bring the material up to date by incorporating some account of the work done since the earlier publication. This has meant that some chapters have been almost completely re-written; others, which deal with subjects that inspired little research during the past decade, are scarcely altered. But archaeological research goes steadily on and advances to knowledge are constantly being made so that a book of this type cannot remain up to date. Even as the text goes to press one learns of some new fact to which one would like to refer. That this is so is a tribute to the workers in Irish archaeology. It means, however, that the reader who wishes to keep abreast of research in the subject must attend to the periodical literature as published by archaeological societies (local and national) and learned institutions. If this book causes an increased awareness of these publications as well as of the field monuments here described it will have served a useful purpose.

A word must be said of the chapter headings. These, in some cases, do not fully indicate the extent of the material contained in the chapters. Thus 'Forts' covers such subjects as 'linear earthworks', 'roads', 'fields' and other related matters. This is done to avoid having a multiplicity of short chapters or unwieldy omnibus titles. It is hoped that the use of sectional headings will provide a convenient guide for the reader.

Dublin,   Seán P. Ó Ríordáin
   October, 1952

ACKNOWLEDGEMENTS

I have pleasure in offering thanks to all those who so generously lent blocks or supplied photographs for the illustrations here reproduced; indebtedness for individual items is indicated in the list of plates. My thanks are due to the friends who helped with the surveying of earthworks or supplied the sections on Fig. 1. Indebtedness to the published work of colleagues is shown to some extent in the bibliography but many assisted by supplying unpublished information. In an especial way the chapter on 'Megalithic Tombs' owes much to Mr. Ruaidhri de Valera who helped with information and by discussion and who kindly supplied the plans of tombs on Figs. 3, 4, and 5. The chapter on 'Ancient Cooking Places' benefits from the recent and yet unpublished findings of Professor M. J. O'Kelly. For very considerable help in the work of producing this edition I am most grateful to Miss Máire Mac Dermott.

MAP OF IRELAND

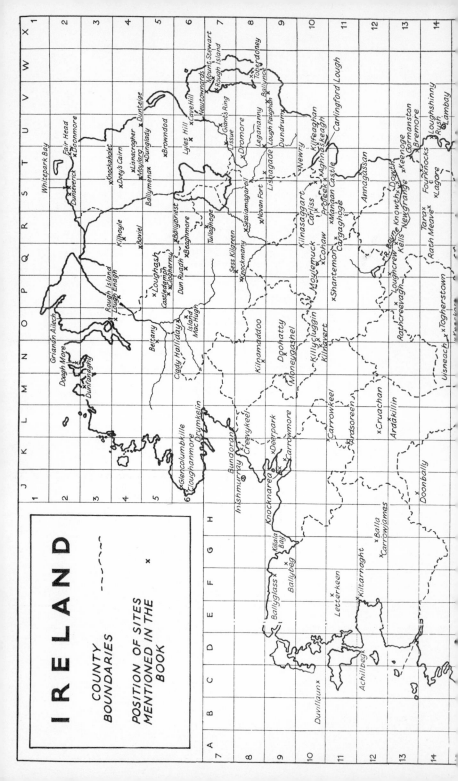

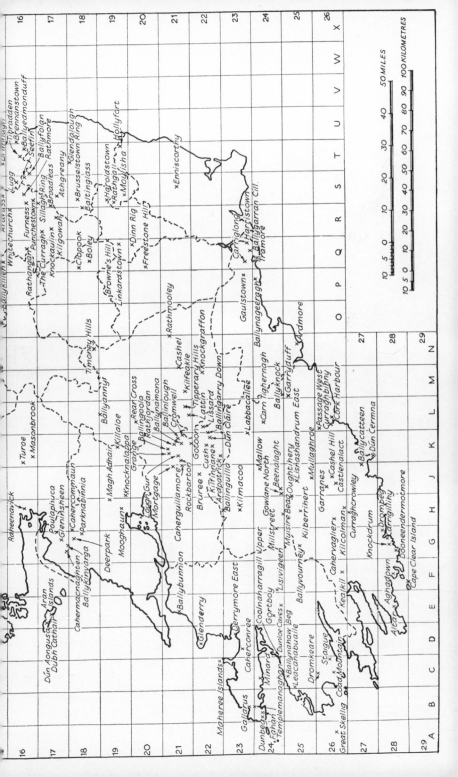

FORTS

We begin with forts not because they have any claim to chronological priority—the order in which the different types of monuments are dealt with has no such significance—but because the structures popularly known as forts are at once the most numerous and the most widely distributed of any class of ancient monument in Ireland. The word fort is used as a general term because it is known throughout the country and is current in archaeological literature, even for structures that have no defensive character in a military sense. In a more specific sense we shall use the term 'ring-fort' for the ordinary forts and shall indicate that certain larger examples (hill-forts) must be regarded as a separate class.

Estimates of the number of forts of earth and stone in Ireland vary from about thirty thousand to over forty thousand. It is *Number* not possible in the absence of a complete archaeological survey to state the exact number of these structures. On the one hand some circular sites indicated on the Ordnance Maps in a manner similar to the ring-forts are in fact other types of monuments; while many small ring-forts have been omitted on the maps. It must suffice, therefore, to say that the number of forts runs into tens of thousands and that examples of them may be found in almost every part of the country, though they are sparse or completely absent in the more inhospitable mountain areas.

In its simplest form the ring-fort may be described as a space, most frequently circular, surrounded by a bank and fosse (3). *Definition* The bank is generally built by piling up inside the fosse the material obtained by digging the latter. In stony districts there may be a stone-built wall instead of an enclosing bank, and there is frequently no fosse in such cases (5, 9). The fosse may be dug in rock, and the broken rock so obtained piled up to form a bank as in the manner of the earthen banks. It may, however, be given a regular stone-built facing on both sides with rock-debris forming the core of the wall. When such a wall has collapsed and when vegetation has grown over it, it is frequently, until excavated, quite indistinguishable from an earthen structure. The material does, however, provide a basis for segregating forts into two broad classes—earthen and stone-built—which classification is reflected in the popular nomenclature, but, as we shall see presently, this classification by material includes numerous variants in the matter of size, nature, and complexity of defences, shape, subsidiary structures, and other features.

Forts are referred to under various Irish terms, and these, or Anglicized versions of them, we frequently find incorporated in place-names: *lios, ráth, cathair, caiseal, dún.* Of these *Names* *lios* and *ráth* are usually applied to earthen forts while *cathair* and *caiseal* are used for stone-built examples. *Dún* is less general and tends to occur in place-names to designate large forts and especially the promontory forts with which we shall deal below. The words *ráth* and *lios* (Anglicized 'rath' and 'liss') are now employed in parts of the country as interchangeable terms to signify an earthen ring-fort. A study of the distribution of these words as elements in place-names shows *ráth* to occur almost exclusively over part of the eastern portion of Ireland while *lios* is more usual elsewhere. The evidence provided by early texts, however, reveals a distinction now lost and shows that *ráth* signified the enclosing bank while *lios* meant the open space between this and the house within. In places where the use of the Irish words has been abandoned these structures are most frequently referred to as 'forts', though the word 'mote' is used in some areas—particularly in Co. Limerick. It must, however, be noted that the popular use of this word is rather indiscriminate and we find that 'mote' is applied to various types of earthen structures.

Ring-forts vary very considerably in size. The diameter of the enclosed space may be only 50 or 60 feet or may be as much as 200 feet. In the more elaborately defended examples *Size* the defences take up a much greater area than that of the enclosure. A triple-ramparted fort may have an external diameter of about 400 feet, while the inner space is only 150 feet in diameter. Examples larger than this are uncommon, though we find, as a distinct class, enclosures usually of much greater size which are termed hill-forts and which will be dealt with below.

The building and occupation of ring-forts extended over a

very long period. The earliest evidence for the fully developed earthen type is provided by the site excavated at Cush, Co.

Dating Limerick. Here, in a series of small ring-forts, conjoined to form two main groups, one of the forts was found to have been utilized as a cemetery when it had gone out of use as a habitation site. Several of the burials were contained in Late Bronze Age urns (76). The conclusion was that this fort (and an adjoining one was found to have been constructed before it) dated from sometime before the end of the Late Bronze Age. While the absolute date in this case has been the subject of discussion there is no doubt of the fact that the ring-fort with enclosing ditch and bank was used as a habitation before the outgoing of the Bronze Age.

This result gives rise to the question of the origin of this type of structure, and, since no good evidence has been given of

Origin prototypes abroad, we are inclined to see it as a native development. Recent excavations give us hints that this conclusion is correct. At Knockadoon, Lough Gur, there are enclosures defined by two concentric circles of upright stones. These sites were formerly regarded as stone circles (ritual sites) but there is clear evidence from the excavation of some of them that they were habitation sites where the space around a house was enclosed by a wall of which only two concentric rows of low upright stones now remain. Originally the wall must have been completed by building a bank of sods between the uprights. That these sites developed in the Early Bronze Age is shown by the large amount of domestic pottery and other finds of that period which they have produced. Also dated by its pottery to the Bronze Age, and probably to an early stage in it, is a site at Carrigillihy, Co. Cork (6). Here the enclosing wall was of stone of peculiar construction, the smaller stones being held in position and given stability by uprights which were set with the long axis placed radially. An oval stone-built house stood within this wall. (A rectangular house was built later—when the rampart was in collapse.)

These early beginnings show us different methods of enclosing a space around a house and this is the fundamental idea embodied in the ring-forts, which were still being built long after the Bronze Age. Occupation on the Cush site continued to the first century of our era or later. Other excavated forts give evidence of later occupation: Turoe, Co. Galway, Early Iron Age; Uisneach, Co. Westmeath, about second century

Late A.D.; Garranes, Co. Cork, about 500 A.D.; Ballycatteen,
examples Co. Cork, somewhat similar in structure and excavated material to Garranes, about a century later; Togherstown, Co. Westmeath, probably sixth century; Letterkeen, Co. Mayo, seventh century; Garryduff, Co. Cork, about the same period; stone fort at Cahercommaun, Co. Clare, eighth century; stone forts at Carraig Aille (Lough Gur), Co. Limerick, eighth to the eleventh century; earthen fort at Lissue, Co. Armagh, tenth and eleventh centuries. While this is the latest date for which excavation has produced clear evidence, historical data suggest that the forts were occupied at an even later period. The fort at Cahermacnaghten, Co. Clare was inhabited by the O'Davoren family and their law school towards the end of the seventeenth century. Medieval pottery (fourteenth century) was found in the fosses of Corliss Fort, Co. Armagh, and pottery of fifteenth–seventeenth century date was found in Ballycatteen fort though this was probably not due to actual occupation. Chance finds reported as having been discovered in unexcavated forts date from all periods from Bronze Age to Medieval times, but in many cases it is not clear if these finds were really associated with the forts.

Excavation has given considerable information as to the purpose of the forts. It must be explained that on a site where

Purpose there were not stone houses but only wooden ones the archaeologist is able, by careful excavation technique, to find evidence of their existence. This is usually done by finding the post-holes of the posts which supported the wooden houses. While nothing of the posts themselves remains (unless in exceptionally favourable—usually wet—conditions) the holes are revealed as pockets filled with a soil which is different from the clay in which they were dug. The fill is usually darker because it contains more humus than the surrounding clay due to the lower ends of the posts having decayed in the holes; but if the posts were removed in ancient times the fill may not be different in colour but only less compacted, in which case the post-holes are found by feeling for the softer areas. Even quite small stake-holes can be found in this way. On some sites the house plan is not revealed by post-holes but by the dark bands which mark the position of house-walls or the burnt clay surface which is all that remains of a wood and wattle house destroyed by fire. As has already been mentioned incidentally, the forts excavated have shown that they enclosed houses—of stone or wood. In one case (Carraig Aille) the fort was the centre of a settlement, there being houses outside the rampart as well as those enclosed by it. At Garranes and Ballycatteen the inhabitants took advantage of the bank on the western or south-western side as shelter from the prevailing wind, and the area of habitation was virtually confined to this portion of these forts. The evidence of occupation on the last two sites was meagre in relation to the size of the enclosures and the same is true to a greater degree of Raheenavick, Co. Galway. This fact and the strength of the banks would indicate that the larger ring-forts did serve as defensive structures—centres into which the population might be gathered in time of danger.

It may be accepted, however, that the large majority of the forts had no real military significance, but were, rather, the protective structures around early farmsteads. Some measure of defence for the occupying family was provided by the banks and fosses within which also cattle might be brought for safety from wolves. It is possible that the tops of the earthen ramparts were strengthened by the erection of wooden palisades, but excavation has not given proof of this, due perhaps to the fact that the summits of the banks have been denuded by time, so removing any evidence of settings for the palisades. A trench for a very strong palisade was found inside the inner bank at Ballycatteen.

Provision for defence in ring-forts is a matter of degree. There are at the one extreme the well-defended sites with high banks (2), deep fosses or (if of stone) well-built walls and other defensive features. At the other end of the scale are sites with one slight bank and a shallow fosse. As already indicated these latter sites had no military significance, but their defences, even when most insignificant, must have given the farmer and his family who lived in them some feeling of security. It is difficult, therefore, to say where to draw the line between the defensive and non-defensive site when all are enclosed to some degree.

Similarly, with buildings of later historic times it is difficult to draw a line when one considers the functions of the strong castle, the tower-house, the imitation castle, and the Georgian house. The strong castle was inhabited by the Norman lord and his family but its purpose was largely military, the Georgian house was domestic in purpose but the steel shutters and other features that were frequently incorporated gave a measure of security.

As stated, the houses enclosed by the forts were of stone or wood and they were round or rectangular in plan. Not all *Houses* excavated forts gave good house plans; sometimes repairs caused a multiplicity of post-holes which could not be intelligibly interpreted, sometimes soil conditions are not suitable for the preservation of the evidence of wooden buildings. The fort excavated at Leacanabuaile, near Caherciveen, Co. Kerry, enables us to form a good picture of one of these sites in an approximately complete state (7). The stone walls of the houses, covered by collapsed material and debris, were found to remain to a height of several feet. Near the middle of the fort were a round and a rectangular house with communicating doorway, while subsidiary buildings stood against the rampart. A site in a marshy area at Grange, Co. Limerick, consisted of a low bank and fosse surrounding a single small wattle hut which had been built on a clay layer thrown up over the peat. On the clay surface the colour changes caused by the burning of the hut clearly indicated its outline (4). The Bronze Age sites mentioned at Knockadoon, Lough Gur and at Carrigillihy, Co. Cork, gave a similar picture of a single house surrounded by an enclosing rampart. The fort at Letterkeen, Co. Mayo enclosed two round houses, one revealed by a circle of post-holes, the other by stone slabs which formed the wall footing.

Excavation is not always necessary to reveal the remains of the enclosed houses. In many of the forts in stony areas the stone-built houses may be clearly traced (17). This is true of numerous stone forts in Co. Clare, in Co. Kerry, on the Aran Islands, and elsewhere. On earthen sites also the outline of an enclosed house is sometimes visible on the ground surface, especially when the conditions of vegetation are favourable. The position of the hut on the Grange site just mentioned was noted before excavation. On the fort marked on the Ordnance Map, as 'Teach Cormaic' at Tara, the outline of a rectangular house is clearly visible. Of course, the house noted on the surface may be only the latest building on a site where excavation would reveal successive houses. On a platform-type ring-fort at Ballingarry Down, Co. Limerick (27), a rectangular house on top was found to be of Norman date but was the successor to several houses of different type at lower levels.

A word must be said of a recent theory based on excavations of ring-fort sites on the Isle of Man. These excavations have *Isle of Man sites* prompted the theory that the bank of a ring-fort did not surround a free-standing house but was, in fact, the collapse of the clay piled as support against the house-wall, the whole area inside the bank being roofed over. The sites investigated had a diameter of about 90 feet inside the bank and concentric rings of post-holes are believed to have held the posts which supported the roof and which divided a central domestic area from outer spaces given over to workshop activities and to livestock. Because of the large diameter the pitch of the roof could not be very great, as a steep pitch would involve the use of impossibly large posts near the centre. It is, therefore, suggested that the disadvantage of the slight slope of the roof was overcome by covering it with sods. Whatever the correctness of this theory for the Isle of Man sites, it is certain that the excavated Irish ring-forts cannot be given a similar interpretation and the literary evidence is also against it. The fort excavated at Lissue, Co. Armagh, is said to have been covered with this type of over-all roof but the evidence is not unequivocally in favour of this.

Many of the Irish ring-forts possess underground chambers known as souterrains with which we shall deal in another *Wall-chambers* section. Chambers are also incorporated in the wide ramparts of some of the stone-built forts—as in Leacanabuaile and Staigue, Co. Kerry and Grianán Ailech, Co. Donegal. In the promontory fort of Dunbeg, Co. Kerry these chambers formed shelters for sentries and were part of an elaborate defensive system. These features, cells and long chambers in the walls are found also in the stone forts and brochs of Scotland, which are known to have been built during Early Iron Age times and were occupied during the period of Roman rule in Britain and later. There seems every reason for supposing that the Irish stone forts began at an equally early date though excavation has not yet confirmed this. With the exception of the early attempts of Bronze Age date and in a different building technique (Knockadoon and Carrigillihy) the earliest dating yet available for an Irish stone ring-fort is in Early Christian times.

The entrance to the earthen forts was normally protected by a gate—the post-holes for the large gate-posts having been revealed by excavation on many sites. At Garranes, Co. Cork, an elaborate series of gates, three (or possibly four) in all, defended the entrance which was a long, comparatively narrow passage between the ends of the banks and fosses. Similarly, multiple gates were used at Ballycatteen, Co. Cork. At both these forts and at Letterkeen, Co. Mayo, the sides of the entrance passage were bordered by a wooden palisade, and at Letterkeen this was continued around the fort outside the fosse. The entrance to an earthen fort was sometimes stone-built—at Cahervaglier, near Coppeen, Co. Cork a gateway formed of upright stone slabs supporting horizontal ones was set in a stone-faced earthen rampart. The entrance to a stone fort may consist simply of a neatly-built gap in the ramparts with perhaps (as at the two forts at Carraig Aille, Lough Gur) recesses in the wall-ends at either side into which fitted the two halves of the wooden gate. More ambitious are the entrances to those high ramparted stone forts such as Staigue (11) and Grianán Ailech where the gateway is an aperture in the wall, lintelled with large slabs, these carrying the upper portion of the wall at this point (8, 15). Of course entrances of this type were probably more numerous than is shown by the extant remains; a collapsed wall will not indicate the upper structure of the entrance.

Other features exemplified by the better-preserved stone forts, such as Staigue, are the 'batter' (inward slope) of the

Structural features

wall-faces, resulting in a narrowing of the wall as it rises, the terracing of the inside of the walls and the provision of steps to give access to these terraces or to the top of the rampart for purposes of defence (12). The rampart would originally have been provided with a

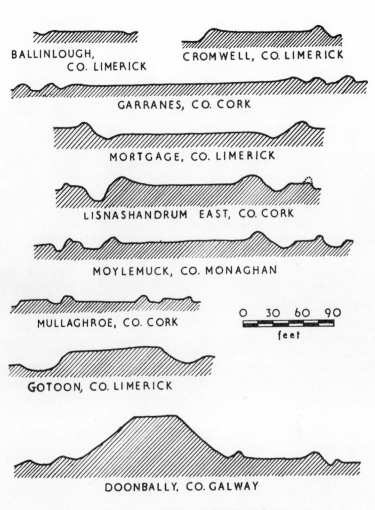

FIG. I. Profiles of Earthworks

Ballinlough: small ring-fort with slight fosse; Cromwell and Gotoon: platform-type; Garranes: triple-ramparted fort; Lisnashandrum, Moylemuck, Mullaghroe: berm between outer bank and inner fosse; Mortgage: fosse *inside* bank; Doonbally: motte-and-bailey.

breastwork to protect those standing on the top. It is hardly necessary to state that mortar is never used in the building of stone forts, but it may be remarked that the quality of their dry-stone building is of a high standard of excellence and shows the ability of the ancient builder to make the most of the type of stone available locally, be that thin slabs of shale or large blocks of limestone. Straight joints in the walls of some of the forts (Cahercommaun, Co. Clare and Staigue) (13) indicate gaps which gave the workers access to the interior during building and the filling of which was the last part of the work.

The number of ramparts with accompanying fosses (Fig. 1) around an earthen fort may vary from one to three, or rarely (as

Defences
at Dunglady, Co. Derry) to more than three. It must be realized that these defences as they exist today are much less imposing than they were in their original state. In the course of time the height of the bank has been considerably reduced by slip and the material from it has fallen into, and to a large extent filled up, the fosse. Excavation shows that the original bottom of a fosse may be covered by 5 or 6 feet of spill—possibly by an even greater amount in some larger forts. In many instances it has been found that the fosses were cut in solid rock, involving in the construction of the larger forts a considerable amount of labour and demonstrating the high degree of social organization which made such concentrated effort possible. Usually in forts with multiple defences the fosses and banks were constructed contiguously—there being no space between them. In some forts, generally those with two banks and fosses, a level space intervenes between the outer bank and the inner fosse. This may be referred to as a berm (a term borrowed from military defensive works), and was evidently intended as a platform on which the defenders of the outer bank could stand. We find it at the fort at Lisnashandrum East, Co. Cork, and it is a frequent feature of the forts on the summits of small hills in the Cavan-Monaghan drumlin country. In these, the bank outside the berm is much lower than the inner bank and sometimes has no outer fosse.

As has already been indicated there are forts which are intermediate in type between the two groups definitely

classifiable as of earth or of stone. In some examples, the facing
of the bank is of stone—on one or both sides—while the body of
the bank is of earth or rubble. This is particularly true in the
less stony districts, but even in the areas where stone is plentiful
the best stones are retained for the facings of the rampart
which are excellently constructed while the core is little more
than a loose filling. Fosses accompany some of the stone-built
sites but the majority of the stone forts are built without a
surrounding fosse. In fact the stone forts are most abundant
in rocky areas, such as the limestone of Co. Clare, where the
cutting of a fosse would be a very difficult matter.

Some of the large forts, for instance those on the Aran
Islands (14), have a series of defences which are separated by as
much as several hundred feet and the defensive system is further
elaborated in a few instances by placing outside the walls of the
fort a series of closely set upright stones—known as a *chevaux
de frise* (derived from a military term which originated when
the Frisians used spikes to impede enemy cavalry). This device,
the ancient equivalent for anti-tank traps, occurs in the Aran
Islands and at Ballykinvarga, Co. Clare (16).

While most ring-forts will be found in upland areas, they
occur frequently in low-lying country. They are well represented
in the more marshy districts of the Limerick plain,
Water-filled where they are numerous though very incon-
fosses spicuous. The interior is frequently raised above
the level of the surrounding area, clearly as a
means of achieving a comparatively firm and dry surface. It is
probable that the fosses of these structures contained water.
There also occur in the Co. Limerick marshlands, and perhaps
elsewhere, forts in which the fosse is *inside* the bank. Some of
these have water-filled fosses at present and this would have
been true in most cases when they were constructed. It has been
suggested that these earthworks, none of which has been
excavated, were intended as cattle enclosures, for which purpose
the fosses would have provided a convenient water-supply.
This suggestion, which may be correct, runs counter to the
general rule that sites with the fosse inside the bank are usually
ritual in purpose. We know, however, of ritual sites with the
fosse on the outside and it is not necessarily true that all those
with the bank on the outside were non-utilitarian in purpose.

The fosses in the majority of the upland forts would not have contained water, though it seems likely that they did, in some cases, by accident or design. A fine example at Rathmooley, near Killenaule, Co. Tipperary, still has a considerable amount of water in the fosse, probably supplied by springs in the rock in which it was cut. A water-supply for domestic purposes was not included within the enclosure of the forts—exceptions to this are very rare.

It must not be thought that all the forts are circular though this is true of the majority. Square, rectangular, D-shaped and other outlines occur (1). It has been suggested *Rectangular* that the rectangular forts are later than the circular *sites* ones. This need not necessarily be true since we know that the excavation of a small rectangular earthwork, not unlike our forts in character, at South Lodge Camp, Dorset, gave evidence of a Late Bronze Age dating. A large (70 yards across) rectangular enclosure at North Treveneague, Cornwall, is similar to Irish forts even in possessing a souterrain and produced Early Iron Age material.

On the other hand many of our rectangular enclosures may be the sites of 'moated houses' usually attributed to the later *Moated* Middle Ages (fourteenth century onwards). On these *houses* the house stood near the water-filled moat, and the bank was frequently built on the *outside*. They are common in England and occur occasionally on the eastern fringe of Wales. They are best exemplified in this country by examples in Co. Wicklow. A good specimen is to be seen at Whitechurch, near Straffan, Co. Kildare.

Pairs of forts conjoined in the form of a figure-of-eight are not uncommon. More rare are groups containing greater *Conjoined* numbers of conjoined forts; the main group at Cush, *forts* Co. Limerick, consisted of six small conjoined forts with an attached rectangular enclosure. Such enclosures have been brought to notice elsewhere, for instance in connexion with the remains at Cruachan, Co. Roscommon. On the Cush site the enclosure represented the expansion of the settlement and the enclosing of a larger space in which houses were built. In other cases, the enclosures may be more simply explained as the fields accompanying the settlement; again to quote the Cush site, a system of ancient fields was found there in connexion with the forts and was proved by excavation to be coeval with their habitation.

Attached
enclosures
Near the stone forts (Early Christian Period) at Carraig Aille, Lough Gur, were vestiges of field banks which were possibly contemporary with the forts. Certainly contemporary with the hut-site of similar date—the 'Spectacles', Lough Gur (37)—were fields enclosed by stone-faced banks. In the neighbourhood of some early monasteries old fields can be seen—as at Ardpatrick, Co. Limerick or at Donaghmore, near Maynooth, Co. Kildare.

Mention of these fields causes us to digress for a moment to the subjects of fields, roads, and linear earthworks, which,

Fields
though they do not properly fall under the heading of this section, are of considerable interest. The field-worker may hope to find hitherto undiscovered ancient field systems (not necessarily connected with forts or other antiquities) in many parts of the country, particularly on upland areas that have not been enclosed by modern field fences. These ancient field systems will reveal themselves as low banks and the enclosed fields will possibly prove much smaller than their modern counterparts. Of course, the question of date must remain unresolved in most cases. In many places there are abandoned fields which are not earlier than the nineteenth century when land hunger led to the tillage of mountainous parts of the country. Near these are frequently to be seen the ruins of the small houses of the farmers who lived there when the population was much larger than at present. These vestiges of fields and houses are material on which the methods of study of the archaeologist should yield results of value to the social and economic historian.

Terraces
Other evidences of ancient husbandry are cultivation terraces (usually edged by large stones) on hill-sides or in sloping valleys. Such terraces are found in the valley under Knockfennel Hill north of Lough Gur, but their date is not known. Small-scale terracing occurs there also on Knockadoon and is connected with the neigh-bouring Neolithic and Bronze Age habitations. Large long fields bounded by low banks, which appear clearly in certain lighting conditions only, run over Knockfennel. Low field-walls have been found in the Foyle basin on hill-sides from

which the peat has been cut and have been noted to enclose large areas. A feature of some old stone-built walls is the incorporation in them of upright stones; the partial removal of the walls, leaving the upright stones in position accounts for some examples of standing stones and stone alignments. Ancient roads or pathways may occur in connexion with early field systems as at Caherguillamore, Co. Limerick (18) (Medieval site) or quite independently of them, and they offer an interesting subject for anyone with a love of the open country and a flair for the use of maps. Such roads he will find very incompletely recorded, if at all, and the exercise of marking them on the 6-inch Ordnance Maps should prove interesting and instructive. The historian may be able to provide historical data for the identification of some of the ancient roadways, but it will usually be found that historical references *Roads* are hardly detailed enough to allow of their being unambiguously connected with the archaeological findings. Remains of roads may be short stretches which have a local significance or the shorter portions may be part of greater lengths which connected ancient centres—as the Rian Bó Phádraig which is said to have connected Cashel and Ardmore. There are several other instances of names of animals being attached to roads and linear earthworks. The Race of the Black Pig on the Curragh, Co. Kildare, is not a road in the ordinary sense. Sections cut across it showed that it consisted of a trench with slight banks at the sides. It appears to have been similar to so-called 'hollow-ways' found on the English downlands; these served as cattleways linking one pasture with another.

Rather similar to the problem of ancient roads is that of linear earthworks which formed the boundaries or the defensive frontier of territorial divisions. A famous example *Linear* is the Black Pig's Dyke which is to be found inter*earthworks* mittently between the neighbourhood of Newry, Co. Down and Bundoran, Co. Donegal, and which has shorter subsidiary earthworks associated with it. On the line of the Black Pig's Dyke is the enormous oval enclosure known as the Dorsey in southern Armagh. These great works are said to have been built by the Ulstermen to defend their southern frontier—inspired by the example of the Roman wall

1   FORT AT ARDSOREEN, CO. SLIGO

2   INNER FOSSE, BALLYCATTEEN FORT, CO. CORK

3 RING-FORT AT GRANGE, CO. LIMERICK

4 BURNT OUTLINE OF HUT IN GRANGE RING-FORT

5 STONE FORT AT MONEYGASHEL, CO. CAVAN

6 RECONSTRUCTION OF STONE FORT WITH OVAL HOUSE AT CARRIGILLIHY,
CO. CORK

7   STONE FORT AT LEACANABUAILE, CO. KERRY——ENTRANCE AND HOUSES
IN INTERIOR

8   ENTRANCE TO STONE FORT, DÚN AONGUSA, ARAN ISLANDS, CO.
GALWAY

9 STONE FORTS AT CARRAIG AILLE, LOUGH GUR, CO. LIMERICK

10 TARA: "TEACH CORMAIC" AND THE "FORRADH"

11 STONE FORT AT STAIGUE, CO. KERRY

12 WALL STEPS IN INTERIOR, STAIGUE

13 WALL-JOINT AND FOSSE, STAIGUE

14 DÚN AONGUSA, ARAN: STONE FORT ON CLIFF OVER
ATLANTIC

15 PROMONTORY FORT AT DUNBEG, CO. KERRY
—ENTRANCE FROM OUTSIDE

16 STONE FORT AT BALLYKINVARGA, CO. CLARE, SHOWING *chevaux de frise*

17 DUBH CATHAIR, ARAN—WALL-TERRACES AND HUTS IN INTERIOR OF
FORT

18 AERIAL PHOTOGRAPH CAHERGUILLAMORE, CO. LIMERICK, SHOWING
ANCIENT FIELDS, ROADS, FORTS AND HOUSES

19   THE DANGAN PROMONTORY FORT, ACHILLBEG, CO. MAYO

20 HILL-FORT, KNOCKAULIN, CO. KILDARE

21   ENTRANCE TO PROMONTORY FORT, CAVE HILL, CO. ANTRIM

22   FOSSE OF PROMONTORY FORT, LAMBAY, CO. DUBLIN

23 MOTTE-AND-BAILEY, TIPPERARY HILLS, CO. TIPPERARY

24 MOTTE-AND-BAILEY, RATHCREEVAGH, CO. WESTMEATH

25   MOTTE-AND-BAILEY, DROMORE, CO. DOWN

26 MOUND AT MAGH ADHAIR, CO. CLARE

27 PLATFORM-TYPE RING-FORT, BALLINGARRY DOWN, CO. LIMERICK—
DURING EXCAVATION

28 RATH MEAVE, TARA, CO. MEATH

29 KILFINNANE, CO. LIMERICK

in Britain. Such a great earthwork could hardly have been effectively manned in a military sense but it would have served as a deterrent to cattle-raiding. A similar function must have been served by the Pale, a late earthwork of much less imposing character built around the area of the same name. The Claidhe Dubh in East Cork is also unimpressive, in places hardly distinguishable from a normal field fence. It is certain that examples of such ancient boundary banks occur in many parts of the country and are by no means all known to archaeology. Their elucidation presents problems as fascinating as those of the ancient roadways.

Mention has already been made of hill-forts—a class of antiquity distinct from the more usual ring-fort and much less common in Ireland. We have seen that many *Hill-forts* ring-forts occur on hill-tops, and this is especially true of the larger examples and is a feature of their siting in some areas (as Cavan-Monaghan); but while the ring-fort may be placed on the hill-top, the hill-fort encircles the summit, its defences tending to follow the contour. The hill-fort is frequently enormous in size, enclosing as much as twenty acres within its defences which may consist of stone-built rampart or bank and fosse. These hill-forts are presumably related to those in Britain which are of Iron Age date. The British hill-forts served as strong centres in pre-Roman times; most of those in lowland Britain were abandoned as a result of Roman policy soon after the invasion, though sites in the highlands of Wales and elsewhere were built and occupied well into Roman times. In Ireland only one hill-fort has been excavated—at Freestone Hill, Co. Kilkenny—and here the dating evidence was of the fourth century A.D. But at Navan fort, near Armagh, finds of first-century date have come to light—a date which would accord with the historical testimony regarding the great period of this site—ancient Emain Macha, the royal seat of Ulster. At this hill-fort the bank is outside the fosse, a peculiar feature which is repeated at Knockaulin—the ancient Ailenn, a residence of the Leinster kings—near Kilcullen, Co. Kildare (20). Again, at Tara, the great enclosure known as Ráth na Riogh (the fort of the kings) has the bank on the outside. It has been suggested that at Tara this is a ritual feature, since ritual was an important element of Tara's function. But at Navan fort and at Knockaulin the defences, which are built on steep hill-slopes, are effective against attack and a ritual explanation is unnecessary and is probably unnecessary also at Tara.

Other hill-forts are Cashel Hill near Upton and Carn Tighernagh, near Fermoy, both in Co. Cork; Rathgall, Baltinglass Hill, and Brusselstown Ring, all in Co. Wicklow; Mooghaun, Co. Clare, Grianán Ailech, Co. Donegal and smaller examples at Clopook and Boley in Leix. At Clopook a stone wall (with hut-sites inside) encloses the top of a steep-sided knoll; the Boley fort is less impressive—an earthen bank on a low hill. At Rathgall and Grianán Ailech the hill-forts have at their centre a strong stone fort. At Carn Tighernagh, Baltinglass, and Freestone Hill, the summit of the hill was crowned with a cairn, that at Baltinglass containing megalithic tombs. The cairn at Freestone Hill (of Bronze Age date) had no connexion with the hill-fort that happened to have been built on the same hill at a much later date. We may take it that the same is true of Baltinglass and Carn Tighernagh, the desire for a hill-top position being common to the builders of the cairns and the hill-forts. But one large hill-top enclosure, Lyles Hill near Belfast, which had also a cairn at the centre gave a different and surprising result. A layer immediately under the cairn yielded large quantities of Neolithic pottery and similar pottery came also from the bank (there is no fosse) of the enclosure; the burials in the cairn were of Early Bronze Age date. The great stone-built hill-fort at Mooghaun, Co. Clare, is one of our most remarkable antiquities. It has three great stone walls of which the outermost, oval in outline, measures 1,500 by 1,000 feet. In it and on its walls stone ring-forts were built—evidently with the material of the earlier structure. The famous 'Great Clare Find' of gold objects of Late Bronze Age date was discovered when the railway was being constructed in this neighbourhood in 1854 and it has been suggested that this, the greatest of our gold finds, belonged originally to Mooghaun, the greatest of our forts. There is, however, nothing to substantiate this attractive theory. There are enclosures which are not contour forts and which are, nevertheless, too big to be included with the ring-forts. These may be on high ground, though not enclosing a hill-top, as is

Rath Meave (28), near Tara, or on a hill-slope as is Dún Cláire on the foot-hills of the Ballyhouras in Co. Limerick. The Sillagh Ring, south of Naas, Co. Kildare, is also on a hill-slope and is incomplete either because of partial destruction or, more probably, because its builders left it unfinished. Sites like these, though not fully conforming to the hill-fort type, are more closely related to the hill-forts than to the ring-forts, and similar structures would be described as hill-forts in Britain, though far removed from the greatest examples. This problem of classification indicates that a completely satisfactory nomen-clature is not yet available though it is preferable to use terms which have gained currency than to try to force a new terminology which might not only prove unsatisfactory but would also sound artificial. Further, border-line examples will always remain difficult to classify, but serve as a warning against over-simplification. While hill-forts are in general a distinct class probably introduced into the country in Iron Age times, there is no reason why the already developing native ring-fort type should not in some instances have been enlarged to give analogous structures.

A special type of defensive structure is the promontory fort, the name of which is almost self-explanatory. Economy of effort in the enclosing of a large area is achieved by *Promontory* building the defences across the narrow neck of a *forts* sea-girt promontory (19, 22) or in some cases across a mountain spur (21). Of the inland promontory forts the most notable is the spectacular site of Caherconree on the mountains near Tralee, Co. Kerry, more than 2,000 feet above sea-level—a triangle of land, steep-sided on two sides and defended on the third by a wall with terraces on the inner face and a bank of stones and earth.

It is likely that promontory forts were built at different times, but the type is an Early Iron Age one. Three examples excavated recently in West Cork yielded no primary dating material but showed structural features similar to those observed in promontory forts of Iron Age date in Cornwall and Brittany. Fragments of Roman pottery have been picked up at the fine promontory fort at Loughshinny, Co. Dublin, but excavation would be necessary to define their relation to the earthwork. Its position on the east coast makes it a promising site where one might hope for Roman remains to help dating, as the strange absence of Iron Age pottery over so much of the country makes chronology extremely difficult. The sites excavated in Co. Cork not only failed to produce dating evidence but also showed very few signs of occupation and it would appear that they can have served only as short-period places of refuge and not as places of ordinary habitation. On one of the excavated sites, Dooneendermotmore, the defences had been considerably modified in the seventeenth century and a dwelling built within it. Advantage was taken of the existence of many promontory forts to build castles within them. A site to which there are very early historical references is Dún Cermna on the Old Head of Kinsale and on this the de Courcys, Norman lords of the district, built a castle. Dunseverick Castle in Co. Antrim is another site with early historical associations and on it also a castle was built.

Something must now be said about a class of defensive work which is not native in character—the Norman motte-and-bailey.

Motte-and-bailey   ('Mote' and 'motte' are both used for these monuments but it seems preferable to use the French 'motte' as an indication of the fact that they are of Norman origin; we have already noted the colloquial use of 'mote' for various types of earthworks. The word 'moat' means, of course, the surrounding fosse or trench.)

The motte is a high flat-topped mound surrounded by a ditch, attached to which and eccentric to it is a space—the bailey—enclosed by a bank and fosse (23, 24). It has long been known that these sites were Norman and that they held the wooden castles, built in the late twelfth and early thirteenth centuries to consolidate the invaders' gains in the areas of the early conquest, and before the stone castles could be erected. The Bayeux Tapestry depicts—in somewhat naïve manner—the erection of a motte and the fighting around a wooden motte-castle. Because mottes fall well into historic times and there is much documentary data regarding their erection, they have tended to escape the attention of the field-archaeologists though details of their construction can only come from excavation. One was investigated recently at Abinger, Surrey; the top had been encircled by a palisade and the corner-posts of a square tower were found at the centre. At Doonmore, Co. Antrim, excavation showed that a rocky eminence had been occupied in the early Norman period. The rock surface had been levelled and surrounded by a palisade with retaining stone

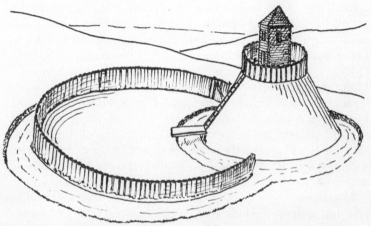

FIG. 2. Reconstruction of a Motte-and-bailey

work, and a terrace at a lower level was bordered by a stone wall. The site, though not a normal motte, gives indications of the same Norman defensive technique.

The wooden tower on the motte (known as a *bretasche*, from which comes the place-name Brittas) served as an observation-post and as a strongly defended position for archers. The motte was usually approached from the bailey by a wooden gangway, though an earthen (or rock) ramp served in some cases or was used as a support for the gangway. In the bailey stood, presumably, the houses of the Norman lord's retainers and into it some, at least, of his cattle might be gathered for safety. It served as an outer line of defence, before retreat to the motte became necessary. The shape of the bailey usually approximates to a half-ellipse, but other outlines are known (25); it may be subdivided by internal banks. The bailey at Knockgraffon, Co. Tipperary, is a large enclosure of irregular outline, divided into separate areas. At this site and also at the neighbouring one of Kilfeakle there are traces of ancient stone buildings. There is sometimes an inner and outer bailey, the latter less well-defended than the former, as at Manaan Castle, Co. Monaghan.

The favourite siting for a motte-and-bailey was on a natural gravel ridge or mound—usually on an esker, but in several instances there are indications either from early *Mottes on* historical references or from finds that the mottes *ancient sites* were built on ancient burial mounds or on other existing earthworks. Knockgraffon is one of the sites mentioned in early historical contexts; at Rathmore, Co. Kildare, burials were found under the motte; at Knockaholet, Co. Antrim (30) and at Sessiamagaroll, Co. Tyrone, a motte was evidently built within an existing ring-fort. A very large ring-fort at Ballykillen near Edenderry, Offaly, has a motte built on the berm-like space between two ditches. On these sites the ancient enclosure served as the bailey of the Norman site. At Knockaholet the motte is placed off-centre in the fort so that space for the bailey is available mainly on one side; at Sessiamagaroll the motte is against the fort bank.

Monuments that would now be accepted as Norman mottes and also others of which there would still be question formed material of a controversy among authorities during the first decade of this century. On the one hand, all Irish structures of the motte class were claimed to be native in origin; the other side, more reasonably, claimed that certain mottes were Norman but, perhaps, did not allow sufficiently for the existence of flat-topped mounds in pre-Norman times.

Such mounds, to which we may refer as 'platform-type ring-forts', are to be found in many parts of the country. Their concentric defences and lack of a bailey dis-*Platform-type* tinguish them from the normal Norman earth-*ring-forts* work, they are sometimes found in non-Norman contexts—on famous early Irish sites. We are not completely dependent on these indications as evidence of the non-Norman character of the platform-type ring-forts. One excavated at Ballingarry Down, Co. Limerick (27), gave evidence of several occupation levels and of successive additions which increased the height of the mound. While a post-Norman house had been built on the top, the important fact is that the flat-topped mound had reached its full height in pre-Norman times—probably as early as the eighth century. Similar mounds must in many cases be of native construction. Within the earthwork known as Ráth na Riogh at Tara are two

ring-forts—the one enclosed by ditch and bank, the other—
conjoined to it—of platform type (10). Similarly the hill-fort at
Emáin Macha encloses a flat-topped mound at the summit of
the hill. The site near Leighlinbridge on the Barrow which
has been identified as Dinn Rig, a residence of the Leinster
kings, is a high, steep-sided, flat-topped mound. The same type
exists at Bruree (the ancient Brug Rig), Co. Limerick. At
Kilfinnane, Co. Limerick, is a splendid example surrounded by
three concentric banks and fosses (29), and it has been suggested
that it is a site named in the Book of Rights, which is a pre-
Norman compilation. A somewhat similar earthwork, ascribed
to a different purpose, is that at Magh Adhair, Co. Clare (26),
the inauguration place of the Dál gCais. Here a flat-topped
mound surrounded by a fosse, across which is a ramp, is
associated with a smaller mound (probably a burial mound)
and standing stones.

Mention of the inauguration place at Magh Adhair brings
to mind other earthworks which in general character resemble
the forts but are known to be ritual sites, not places
of habitation. A well-known example is the so-called
Giant's Ring, near Belfast, where an immense
earthen bank (590 feet in diameter, 15 feet high)
surrounds a flat space at the centre of which is a dolmen (31).
The 'Longstone Rath' at Furness, near Naas—bank with outside
fosse—has at the centre a grave beside a standing stone. In the
bend of the Boyne, where the Brugh na Bóinne cemetery of
chambered tombs is situate, we find, not far from the Dowth
tumulus, a fine fort-like structure surrounded by a single bank
and, apparently, no fosse. It has been suggested that this was a
site where ritual was carried on in connexion with burials in the
cemetery. The suggestion appears reasonable though excavation would be necessary to verify it. It is, perhaps, significant
that there is also an enclosure near the Fourknocks tombs in
the south of Co. Meath. Here the ditch is inside the bank—the
enclosure is likely to have been a ritual one and may well have
served the same function in relation to the neighbouring tombs
as that suggested for the Dowth monument in relation to the
Boyne group.

The presence of a standing stone and a burial monument
has been mentioned at Magh Adhair and at Longstone Rath.

Ritual
enclosures

At Tara, the large enclosure Ráth na Riogh encompasses not only lesser forts but also the burial mound known as the Mound of the Hostages (77), and the standing stone, said to be the Lia Fáil, formerly stood on or near this mound. Undoubtedly Tara was not only a centre of royal residence but also a place of religious importance—the inauguration of the kings being one of the religious ceremonies which were carried on there. Other sites of inauguration or assembly also combined ritual and residential function—to judge by the extant remains. For instance, Tullaghoge, Co. Tyrone, the inauguration place of the O'Neills, appears to have been a triple ramparted ring-fort on a hill-top. The Curragh, Co. Kildare, was an ancient assembly place and is notable for a large number of earthworks —mostly, however, of the bank-outside-fosse type—and something will be said of these in relation to barrows and to 'henge' monuments (connected with stone circles) to which they are related, as are also some of the other ritual sites mentioned here.

A special type of enclosure is dealt with here because of its similarity to the forts. These sites are variously referred to as *cillín, ceallúrach, calltrach* and other variants, and are *Cillíni* marked on the Ordnance Maps under one of these names or as 'Children's Burial Ground' or 'Disused Burial Ground'; the word *cill* and its variants is derived from the Latin *cella* and came to mean a church or graveyard. In general character the enclosure is frequently similar to a ring-fort, being circular—sometimes irregularly so—in outline, but local tradition tenaciously refers to it as a burial site. Until recent times such burial places continued to be used for unbaptized children, and a custom is known relating to a site in Co. Kerry that the first child of a family to die before reaching adult years should be interred in the neighbouring cillín. The bank surrounding a cillín is usually much less well-constructed than that around a fort and has rather the character of the ordinary field fence. Certain of these sites contain the remains of a building, evidently the early church. Excavation at Ballygarran Cill, near Waterford, gave evidence of the existence there of a long rectangular wooden building, presumed to have been a church. A cross-inscribed stone indicated the Christian associations of the place, while a considerable amount of iron slag suggested that ordinary domestic and industrial activity was carried on there. A feature, sometimes found in cillín sites, is the division of the enclosed space into two unequal parts by a dividing wall or bank. The church site may be found in the larger division, while the smaller was reserved for burial (as at Kilcolman, west of Bandon, Co. Cork), but there is no constant rule in this respect and the church is contained in the smaller portion at Duvillaun, Co. Mayo. Ogham stones have frequently been found in cillín sites—in fact these sites have been the most prolific source of ogham stones.

In the 'Lives' of the Irish saints one finds instances where the local chieftain gave over his dún to the missionary who converted him to Christianity. Such occurrences would account for the ring-fort character of the cillín sites, as would also the general fashion of enclosing a site by bank and rampart. The same defensive features are found on normal monastic sites. At Inishmurray, Co. Sligo and at Maheree Island, Co. Kerry, there are massive enclosing stone walls while Templemanaghan, Co. Kerry, is surrounded by an earthen rampart. Hill-top church sites with enclosing banks are a feature of certain areas, for instance, Co. Cavan, and there are examples of large hill-top enclosures with, at the centre, a smaller area which encloses the cemetery and the church or church site—as at Kilmacoo, near Kanturk, Co. Cork. The enclosing bank or wall of the cillín is generally unpretentious, the remains of buildings, when in evidence at all, are slight, while the use of the site for exceptional burial custom (of the unbaptized) is its chief distinguishing feature. The explanation of the difference between the cillín and the ordinary monastic or other early ecclesiastical site is a matter of surmise. The theory has been advanced that cillíns were originally places connected with a pre-Christian cult which were taken over in the early days of Christianity in Ireland and rededicated to the new religion. Again, it has been suggested that they are the result of an early stratum of Christian activity and that there were, 'so to speak, two or more layers or strata of Early Irish Christianity'. The sites are very numerous; it has been stated that one hundred and twenty-six are known in one single diocese in which there were also nearly one hundred early churches which, after the synods of Kells and Rathbreasail, became parish churches.

The cillín remains, therefore, a tantalizing subject of study on which excavation of suitable examples, where burials do not interfere with the main features, would be hoped to throw some light.

Misconceptions in relation to forts have become so firmly implanted in the popular mind that it may not be out of place to deal briefly with them. The most widespread *Popular* is, perhaps, the idea that these structures were *misconceptions* built and inhabited by the Danes. It has been suggested that this is the result of a misunderstanding due to confusing the Danes with the Dé Danann, a people mentioned in the early mythological accounts of the colonization of Ireland. This cannot be a correct explanation; the forts are no more due to the Dé Danann than to the Danes and their attribution to the latter is an old idea. Giraldus Cambrensis writing in the twelfth century spoke of the 'great trenches, very deep and round and frequently in threes, and also walled fortifications (*castella*) still complete but empty and uninhabited' which he ascribed to the Norse under Turgesius. Possibly this passage by Giraldus was noted and accepted by early antiquaries whose speculations were perpetuated by works like Lewis's *Topographical Dictionary*, which has frequent reference to large 'Danish forts'. This in turn came to be quoted by popular writers on local antiquities. (It is general popular usage to refer to the Scandinavian invaders as Danes, though in fact the Norse were far more numerous here.) The speculation of the early antiquaries, being the first in the field, was widely accepted and was disseminated to people otherwise innocent of literary erudition. It is clear from the chronological data we have given that forts were built long before the Norse invasions and continued to be used after them. Some excavated examples were occupied during Viking times and, indeed, Viking material has been found in them, as the Viking silver excavated at Carraig Aille, and that found at Rathmooley, Co. Tipperary. But there is no evidence that the sites are anything other than native ones. Earthwork enclosures of the Viking period are known in Scandinavian countries—great works like those at Trelleborg and Aggersborg in Denmark and at Haithabu in Schleswig-Holstein—and it is possible that the Vikings built promontory forts, perhaps as bridgeheads, in

Ireland. It may be suggested that the promontory fort on the river mouth at Annagassan, Co. Louth, is due to the historically known Norse settlement there. But no fort of Norse construction has yet been verified in Ireland and even if such are found they will not influence the conclusion that the forts in general are due to native activity.

The feature of the forts which most impresses itself on the popular imagination is the existence in them of underground chambers, known to archaeology as souterrains, *Souterrains* with which we shall deal in our next section. To the certainty which is known there is added a vast amount of nebulous belief which has no foundation in fact. There is, for instance, no truth in the suggestion that passages connect one fort with another, and common sense would indicate that in many cases where they are said to exist the construction of such a passage would be a major engineering feat. We have frequently been asked, by visitors to our excavations, if we have found 'the entrance to the fort' while, actually, the entrance—a solid causeway through the fosses—was perfectly clear even before excavation. What the questioner had in mind was the entrance to a souterrain, and questions on our part revealed that to his mind the fort consisted of a vast series of underground rooms. It must be explained that the souterrain usually occupies a comparatively small space in the interior of the fort, and that normal habitation meant the use of houses placed above ground.

Another common belief is that a fort is always so placed as to be in view of one or more other examples—analogous to the Martello towers built around parts of the coast because of the Napoleonic invasion scare and intended as signalling stations to convey alarm signals from one to another. The forts are not so sited. It is frequently possible to see one from another, but this has no more significance than has the fact that there are few farmhouses from which one or more others cannot be seen. In the case of hill-top ring-forts the popular conclusion is easy to understand especially in the drumlin country where the hills are so frequently crowned by forts, but even there no military significance need be attached to the choice of site. It has been argued that the forts east of the Dane's Cast (a linear earthwork near the Down-Armagh border) were constructed as a group to provide defence behind the Cast. This could only be substantiated if a number of the forts were found on excavation to be contemporary and similar in structure. The excavation of one (Lisnagade) was disappointing as it was proved to have been very much altered in modern times and it gave no early dating material.

Still another misconception is the idea that forts were intended as places of burial. We have already mentioned a site (Cush) where burials were found in a fort, but in this instance and in others (such as Turoe, Co. Galway) the fort was used primarily as a habitation and only secondarily for burial. We have also indicated that there are ritual sites similar in general appearance to forts, but these exceptions do not invalidate the rule which must be emphasized—that forts were intended for habitation and not for burial.

SOUTERRAINS

Mention has already been made of souterrains in connexion with forts. In many forts it is possible to surmise that a
Souterrains and forts souterrain exists because subsidence indicates its position and may even show the approximate outline of the structure. In some cases the original entrance or an entrance through the collapsed roof gives access to the souterrain. More usually, however, there are no surface indications and a souterrain comes to notice only as a result of accidental discovery—collapse due to ploughing, quarrying, boys digging for rabbits or such causes. Only a very small proportion of known souterrains has been found as a result of formal excavation. It will therefore be realized that it is not possible to give any accurate estimate of the number of souterrains in the country. The total must be very large—possibly almost as great as that of the forts.

Not every fort contains a souterrain and not all souterrains are enclosed in or connected with forts. The former part of this statement is proved by excavations where the whole area of a fort has been investigated and no souterrain has been found. The latter part of the statement is more difficult to prove, since a souterrain may be found where the fort which once enclosed it has been cleared away without leaving any trace. Close observation in the case of certain souterrains and even trenching of the whole surrounding area in one case—at Ballymena, Co. Antrim—revealed no indication of the former existence of a fort, and there can be no doubt that some of these structures were built independently of forts. Striking examples are the souterrains inserted in the Boyne passage-grave mounds —at the base of the Dowth mound and at the summit of that at Knowth.

A souterrain may be defined as an artificially built cave. It must, therefore, not be confused with natural caves which
Definition occur in limestone areas, and which were, in many cases, used as habitations at different periods. Souterrains are, however, generally marked 'cave' on the Ordnance Map.

The methods of construction of souterrains vary considerably. Some were tunnelled in the clay where this was of such consistency as to allow of its being dug into without danger of collapse. Others were similarly cut in rock, though not in the harder varieties, but in those shales and sandstones where the bedding makes it a comparatively easy task to remove the rock in flakes. These clay or rock-cut souterrains do not incorporate any stone building in their construction, but since the use of this method of building a souterrain is strictly limited by geological factors, we find much more frequently that souterrains have stone-built walls and roof. In these cases, the method generally was to cut the souterrain in the clay, line the cutting with stone-built walls, and roof these walls with cross-slabs. Combinations of these methods are known where part of a souterrain is cut in rock or clay, and part is stone-built (e.g. Kilberrihert, near Aghabullogue, Co. Cork), or we may have a souterrain cut in rock without stone walls, but with a lintelled roof as at Toberdoney, Co. Down. Excavation has shown that some souterrains of the stone-built type, did not have stone roofs but were roofed with timber. Carefully shaped recesses for the upright posts intended to support such a roof were noted at Ballycatteen fort, Co. Cork (32), while some of the souterrains at Cush, Co. Limerick, gave evidence of having been roofed in part with stone and in part with timber. The souterrain at Letterkeen, Co. Mayo, had no stone-built wall, and the roof was supported by posts ranged along the sides.

Construction

A feature of the rock- and clay-cut souterrains is the existence in them of small opes in the walls, now built up with stone, but providing, at the time of construction of the souterrain, a means of removing to the surface, through open shafts, clay, and rock-chips according as they were cut away by the souterrain builders. Other features noted in connexion with these souterrains, and less frequently in the case of stone-built examples, are trenches intended to drain off water, and chimneys connected with hearth sites marked by accumulations of charcoal. These features are well exemplified in the splendid rock-cut souterrain found at Curraghcrowley, near Ballineen, Co. Cork. Ventilation shafts have been noted in souterrains of different

Drains and ventilation

types, and, in some cases, it has been remarked that the end of the shaft was some distance from the souterrain, placed, it would appear, so as to lessen the possibility of its discovery by an enemy, and thus prevent the occupants of the souterrain from being smoked out or otherwise driven forth for lack of air.

Characteristic of souterrains in parts of the North (Co. Down) and West (Co. Galway) of Ireland is an obstruction or trap variously arranged but always directed to the purposes *Traps* of making it easy for a person in the souterrain to defend himself against an unwelcome intruder. In its simplest form, this construction consists of a mound of stones or earth, which, in an already inadequate passage, makes access very difficult. More elaborate forms consist of a slab or wall which rises from the floor, inside which is a second slab or wall built downwards from the roof, there being but a small space between the two slabs. To pass these a person has to wriggle uncomfortably, and would meanwhile be quite defenceless against the occupant of the inner part of the souterrain. In the more labyrinthine examples of the souterrains, blind passages may be incorporated to add to the difficulty of the intruder.

In plan, a souterrain may be comparatively simple or may achieve great complexity. In its simplest form, it consists of a narrow passage, sometimes of considerable length. It is *Plans* more usual, however, to divide up the long passage into a series of chambers connected by tunnels barely large enough to allow a person to pass through them. These tunnels are not merely structural devices but, because of their small size, are a defensive feature in the nature of the obstructions described above. Many souterrains contain beehive-shaped chambers built on the corbelled principle as in the manner of the early chambered tombs (passage-graves) and of the clochán-type huts of the Western seaboard. Though the distribution of the various types of souterrain has not yet been worked out, it has been noted that beehive-chambers exemplifying the corbelled technique are frequent in Co. Meath, where also are found the great passage-graves of Brugh na Bóinne and Sliabh na Caillighe, the chambers of which are built in the same technique. Corbelling to a lesser extent is noted in souterrains which do not possess beehive-chambers, but in which the upper courses of the stone walls project inwards to allow of their span by shorter lintels than would be necessary if the walls were vertical. Examples are known where the chambers are not all on one level but tend, as it were, to form a two-storied structure.

Most known examples of souterrains occur in connexion with forts and it may be remarked that they are to be found in association with many different types of forts, those *Association* of stone and earth, ring-forts, and promontory forts *with forts* —but not with hill-forts. In some cases, the souterrain or souterrains are completely enclosed by the forts, in others there may be an opening outside the fort, as in the case of the promontory fort at Dunbeg, Co. Kerry (33), where the outer end of the souterrain is outside the stone rampart, and again at Cahercommaun, Co. Clare, where one souterrain led to the outer face of the rampart. Cells in the walls of some of the stone forts are constructed in a similar manner to the souterrains, and the souterrain at Leacanabuaile, Co. Kerry, led to a large chamber constructed in the wall.

An unusual use of a souterrain in a now almost obliterated fort is noted at Kiltarnaght, Co. Mayo. Here the partly unroofed souterrain has filled with water to a depth of 3 feet and is resorted to as a holy well ('St. Dominick's Well') at which 'rounds' are made.

When dealing with forts, we remarked that a popular misconception was the idea that a fort consisted of a vast series of underground chambers, and we pointed out that *Extensive* in general the area occupied by a souterrain was *souterrains* only a small proportion of that enclosed by the fort defences. There is, however, some ground for the popular idea in those exceptional cases where very complicated souterrains occupy almost the entire interior of a fort. Such examples are known in Co. Kerry, e.g. at Derrymore East, near Tralee, and it has been said of Co. Antrim that 'whole fields are entirely honeycombed with a mass of these souterrains, forming a kind of underground village'. Very extensive systems such as these are, however, rare, and inadequate exploration has given rise to the popular idea that many souterrains are more extensive and complicated than is actually the case.

It has been mentioned that most known examples of souterrains are connected with forts. Where this is not so,

Surface buildings we may suppose that the souterrain was normally associated with a building above ground. Where such a building was of wood, it has vanished, leaving no trace, and excavation has not yet substantiated the suggestion of its former existence. We do know, however, that souterrains were directly connected with stone-built hut-sites—within a fort as at Knockdrum, near Castlehaven, Co. Cork, or where no fort exists as in the case of the huts at Glenderry, near Ballyheigue, Co. Kerry. It is, however, likely that some souterrains were built apart from any building above ground so that they would the better escape detection.

Enough has been said regarding structural details of souterrains to enable us to discuss their purpose. The presence

Purpose of traps or obstructions in some of them makes it clear that these must have been used as places of refuge and in general we must regard this as the purpose for which many souterrains were intended. They would serve for temporary security during periods of fighting, and the small passages in some of them would seem to indicate that in these cases they provided shelter for the children only. It has been suggested that souterrains found in connexion with early church sites (for instance, one at Glencolumbkille, Co. Donegal) were intended as a substitute for, and to serve the same purpose as round towers—places of temporary security where the church valuables might be stored in time of danger.

This explanation of their purpose (as refuges) does not, however, cover all the possibilities. Accumulations of charcoal,

Dwellings the presence of chimneys and other evidences of occupation demonstrate that certain souterrains must have been used as dwelling-places, however uncomfortable, and not merely as refuges. It is notable that these evidences of habitation are found more frequently in the rock-cut souterrains than in the stone-built ones.

Some souterrains—usually of simple construction—possess neither defensive provisions which would make them suitable as places of refuge nor hearths or other features which would indicate habitation. These examples can hardly have served any purpose other than storage—they were, in fact, primitive

cellars. What commodities were stored in them is a matter
of speculation—perhaps milk or milk products, such as cheese,
Storage   perhaps grain. In this connexion we are reminded of
Caesar's statement that the Celts stored their grain in
underground granaries. The souterrain at Letterkeen,
Co. Mayo, was a simple passage entered at one end where there
was a crude step; it had no elaboration to make it suitable as a
place of refuge and must have served merely for storage. This
is likely to have been true also of some of the Cush souterrains
and the same conclusion has been reached regarding one at
Cave Hill on the outskirts of Belfast. At Carraig Aille, Lough
Gur, a deep square rock-hollow associated with the house-sites
outside one of the forts had evidently been artificially enlarged
and provided with irregular steps so as to serve for storage in
lieu of a normal souterrain.

It is clear, therefore, that a single explanation as to purpose
does not cover all examples of souterrains. Their structural
features show them to have been built for different reasons,
though it is possible that sometimes one might have been
utilized in several ways. It seems likely, however, that there
is a unity of tradition behind the whole of the Irish souterrain
building. The chronology of the different types is not yet known
so that a sequence cannot be established either on the basis of
structure or of function.

Finds in souterrains have not been numerous, and few of
them are of value for purposes of dating. Bronze axes, one a
Finds   palstave (Middle Bronze Age type) and another a
socketed axe (Late Bronze Age) are said to have been
found in a souterrain at Aghadown, near Baltimore,
Co. Cork, and bronze spears are reported from another near
Hollyfort, Co. Wexford. Ogham stones are frequently found
as part of the building material of souterrains—as many as
fifteen were found in a souterrain at Ballyknock, Co. Cork.
This shows that these structures were built at a time, not earlier
than the early centuries of Christianity in this country, when
the ogham stones used in their construction were no longer
regarded with reverence. In the Dunloe 'cave' near Killarney,
ogham stones and a cross-inscribed stone were found incorporated in the structure.

Under the clay and rock-chips thrown up by the builders of

the souterrain at Letterkeen, Co. Mayo, was found a bronze ring-pin assigned to about the seventh century. Souterrains in the North of Ireland have yielded coarse domestic pottery which because of this association has been called 'souterrain ware'; it occurs not only in the souterrains but also in ring-forts, for instance on the tenth–eleventh-century site at Lissue, Co. Armagh. This pottery cannot be very closely dated but appears to survive through a considerable portion of Early Christian times. Medieval pottery appears to have been associated with the souterrain in the Knowth tumulus.

Other references in the published material mention the finds of 'urns' in souterrains but, since the vessels in question are not illustrated, one cannot definitely say if they are really burial urns or merely domestic pottery as already noted. Unequivocal evidence of the early beginnings of these structures is, however, provided by the excavations at Cush, Co. Limerick, which have already been cited in relation to the chronology of ring-forts. The ring-fort that contained the Late Bronze Age burials enclosed also a collapsed souterrain and the position of the burial urns in relation to this showed definitely that the souterrain was earlier than the burials, and had become disused and had collapsed before the interments took place.

On the basis of the evidence at present available we may state that the history of souterrains in this country begins in *Date* Late Bronze Age times but that they continued to be constructed during the Early Christian period and may have been used, if not actually constructed, in Medieval times. Historical references are not as helpful as they might be because of the use of the ambiguous word 'cave'. Thus, when we are told that the Norsemen looted the caves of Munster we do not know definitely if natural caves or souterrains are in question. Again, the looting by the same people of the caves at Dowth and Knowth may refer to souterrains or passage graves. A late historical reference is found in an account of the war of 1641 when large parties of women and children were said to have been smothered or otherwise put to death in caves in Co. Antrim, and since the area has not natural caves, we may accept it that refuge was taken in souterrains with which the area abounds. The numbers of people mentioned—two hundred and twenty in two caves, and sixty-three in another—

are, if accurate, an indication of the extensive size of the souterrains. It may be noted also that some ancient souterrains were used as hiding-places or deposits for 'dumps' of arms during the recent periods of fighting in Ireland, and, in fact, similar structures were constructed for the same purpose.

A word must be said regarding the distribution of souterrains. They are found all over Ireland. They occur in Scotland where they are referred to as *earth-houses* or sometimes as *Distribution*   *weems* (from *uamh*, a cave) or *wags* (from *uaigh*, a grave, vault, or cave). One at Jarlshof, Shetland, was found by excavation to be Early Iron Age in date, and other Scottish examples have the stones of Roman buildings incorporated in their structural material. We find them again in Cornwall where they are known as *fogous* and where the material found in them belongs to the Early Iron Age. Somewhat similar structures are the French *souterrain-refuges*. In Iceland, they are merely rock-cut tunnels, and not built of masonry. At least one example is found in Jutland; it is stone-built and dates from Early Iron Age times. Otherwise they are not found on the Continent and nowhere are they found in such profusion as in Ireland. Their occurrence in Cornwall and in Scotland seems to be due to Irish influence. Their non-occurrence in Wales is a puzzling feature of their distribution in view of the other evidences of Irish connexions there. Where and how the souterrains as a type originated is not yet clear. It has been suggested that they derive from the chambered tombs or megaliths, to be dealt with later in this booklet, but the suggestion lacks proof. One can only say that there is a similarity between rock-cut souterrains and rock-cut tombs as also between the corbelled technique of the stone-built souterrains and that of the great passage graves. Souterrains present fascinating problems, in the elucidation of which the amateur archaeologist can help by planning and describing structures known to him, as our knowledge of the different types of souterrains depends on increasing the number of accurately described examples. In the examination of such structures, the field-worker should, in particular, examine the roofing slabs for ogham inscriptions since many of our ogham stones have been brought to light in this manner.

HOUSE-SITES

Dwellings associated with forts have already been discussed. In many parts of the country remains of dwellings quite independent of forts may be noted. These are *Preservation* referred to as hut-sites or house-sites; the latter term indicates something larger or better constructed than does the former, but there is no definite convention as to the distinctive use of the two terms. It must, of course, be understood that many ancient dwellings which were constructed solely of wood have left no surface indications and their plans can be recovered only as a result of careful excavation technique. Nor are wooden buildings the only ones that may leave no visible remains on the ground. It is instructive to study a deserted mud-walled house, built, perhaps, in the nineteenth century, and to notice how rapidly it disappears when the roof and upper portion of the walls have gone. Even stone walls may be no longer visible if the stone has been removed from all but the lower courses and if these have become covered with debris and vegetation; excavation is then necessary to reveal them. Accidental factors must always play an important part in this matter of the degree of preservation; a suitable spell of weather would allow grass to grow over the partly destroyed walls of a mud-house and this would prevent further erosion, so the walls would remain visible as low banks. Again, even quite low remains of stone buildings will continue to be evident on hill-slopes where the vegetation is not sufficiently vigorous to cover them and where they are not removed for tillage or robbed of their remaining stones.

It must not be thought that the use of wood or stone in house building has necessarily any chronological significance. There are sites—the Neolithic–Early Bronze Age ones on *Stone and* Knockadoon, Lough Gur—where the earliest houses *wood* tended to be largely or completely of wood, while stone was employed to a greater degree in later stages, but in general both materials were used contemporaneously throughout the history of early building. Again, houses were frequently made partly of stone and partly of

35

wood. To some degree building tradition played a rôle in the choice but the relative availability of the two types of material was the chief deciding factor.

Since we deal with remains that may be observed on the ground surface rather than those which are revealed by excavation we shall first look to those stone buildings *Clocháns* of clochán type of which considerable portions or even complete structures remain. These are numerous in the West and South-west of the country—on the coastal mainland and on the islands. Clocháns are built in the corbelled method. Corbelling consists of placing courses of flat stones so that each course, as the building proceeds upwards, projects farther in than the preceding one. Thus the sides tend to meet at the top and the roof is really a continuation of the walls, but may be completed by spanning the opening at the summit by a single large flat stone. To secure stability the walls have to be of considerable thickness in relation to their height. In their simplest form, these buildings are round in plan and are shaped like beehives. This method of building is found also in certain of the chambers of passage-graves and, as already noted, in some of the souterrains. It is a technique known in the Mediterranean area from which it must have reached Ireland at an early date. It continued to be employed almost, if not quite, down to our own day in the construction of out-offices of houses on the Dingle Peninsula (39), though it will be found that the recent builders, less sure of their technique, or for added protection, have frequently completed the structure with a concrete top. Similar clochán-like buildings, presumably erected within the past few centuries, are found over some holy wells. In these mortar was used to bond the stones, and similar combination of corbelling and mortar may be seen, often excellent in execution, in domed portions of our Medieval castles or abbeys. Nor is Ireland the only country where the beehive houses continue into modern times. Villages built in this manner are still inhabited in the 'Heel' of Italy, and certain farm out-buildings so constructed are known in Wales. Corbelled buildings, some of which are remarkably similar to Irish churches of the Gallarus type, occur in Burgundy and other districts in France. While many of these are modern, indications of early beginnings are given by finds of prehistoric and Roman date which have come from others.

A circular plan is by no means the only one used in clocháns, though this was presumably the earliest type. Others are square or rectangular or they may be round externally but square inside, as are the huts of the monks on the Great Skellig Island, Co. Kerry. Groups of multiple clocháns are known and consist of two or more of these structures placed abutting one another (38). The corbelling technique is also used in buildings of which only the walls are believed to have been of stone, the roof having been completed with wood and thatch or other perishable material. The houses in the stone fort at Leacanabuaile were evidently completed in this way—the occurrence of post-holes inside the houses suggests that posts were used to support the roof which rested on the corbelled stone walls.

It is not known clearly how early are the first of the clocháns in Ireland. We know the principle of corbelling to be as early *Dating* as the megalithic tombs, but no evidence is forthcoming to show clocháns to be as old as this. In the early centuries of Christianity in this country, the practice of clochán building was already old, for we find primitive churches built in the developed form of this technique—on a rectangular ground plan. Gallarus, Co. Kerry, is the best known of these churches. It is this corbelling technique, with the use of mortar added, which allows the building of more developed churches with stone roofs such as those at Friars Island, Killaloe, at Kells, and at Glendalough. The stone roof of the early twelfth century of Cormac's Chapel, Cashel, and those of St. Doulagh's north of Dublin and at Ardrass near Celbridge, Co. Kildare, owe something to the same tradition though the method of construction has considerably altered. A splendid example of corbelling is to be found in the lock-up cell attached to Newtownards Town Hall—built about 1770; large stones are used in a manner reminiscent of the passage-graves, but mortar is employed.

The corbel-roofed house has, in any case, a long history in Irish building. It begins at least as early as the end of pre-Christian times and continues to our own day. How much earlier it began, excavation may tell us when a fortunate excavator succeeds in finding early examples of a type of building that has changed but little through long ages. (Unfortunately, the finds from the Leacanabuaile fort with its corbelled houses, could not be closely dated; they probably belong to Early Christian times, but habitation there may have begun in the Early Iron Age.) Excavation has not been called to help to any extent in this problem up to the present and archaeologists have been content to survey clocháns without further investigating them.

Such surveys as have been done have shown how numerous clocháns are in some areas—as in Co. Kerry where the best concentration is known from the Fahan area of the Dingle Peninsula. But many such huts or hut-groups exist in various stages of preservation and have never been brought to notice in the archaeological literature and may not even be recorded on the Ordnance Survey Maps. Their recording and planning would repay the efforts of enthusiastic field-workers.

Other house-sites not of clochán type leave varying classes of surface indications. If stone has been used, it may still be in evidence on the surface, but if it is covered by the *Other* turf the outline of the house may be indicated by *house-sites* low banks only. Stone was used in ancient building in various ways—as uprights forming wall-facings, as foundation course only or as coursed masonry. Attention was drawn to the Neolithic and Bronze Age houses at Knockadoon, Lough Gur, by reason of the fact that large stones, which indicated the house outline, projected over the grass surface (34). Excavation showed that these were merely a foundation course which supported the wall material. The roof and the main body of the walls were supported by wooden posts, so that the stones served only to lift from the ground surface the organic material or sods used to form the walls.

Houses of Early Christian date, round (36) or rectangular in plan, were differently constructed. In these the wall was faced with large stones on both sides between which there was a filling of rubble. Such walls could not have been carried to a great height and were completed with other material or in some cases may have sloped down to rest on the low wall-tops. Medieval dwellings, rectangular in plan, excavated at Caherguillamore, Co. Limerick, showed this same method of wall building with double stone facing (40). An early seventeenth-century farmhouse excavated at Lough Gur, however, had coursed masonry which was certainly usual in more pretentious buildings from a much earlier date.

A group of almost fifty circular structures, defined by low walls about 3 feet thick and consisting of two rings of slabs with a stone filling between, has been noted at Carrow-keel, Co. Sligo. The diameters range from 20 to 42 feet and it is thought that they were the protecting walls within which were erected tents or huts, but some appear to have been the walls of roofed structures. Some of the larger enclosures contain within them smaller enclosures (not placed concentrically). Because of their nearness to the Carrowkeel group of chambered cairns it is considered that they may have been the dwelling-places of the builders of the cairns.

Carrowkeel

Level floor space for a hut built on a steep slope was sometimes achieved by digging back into the hill-side and terracing the area in front with the material so obtained. The surround of upright stones then serves the purpose of revetment as well as that of wall to the hut. An example on Coad Mountain, near Sneem, Co. Kerry, presents a fascinating possibility—it may be the dwelling-place of the ancient copper miners who were active in the vicinity (35). (As well as the modern mining, there is on the mountain one old mine which subsequently became an Early Christian hermit's cell.)

When no stone was used in the construction of an ancient dwelling it may, nevertheless, leave surface indications. This has already been discussed above when dealing with the possibility of recognizable traces remaining from a modern mud-walled house. But, as has also been indicated, stone wall remains may become so covered over that one could not know from surface features only if the visible banks are of clay or stone.

In marshy areas, however, where stone would have been difficult to obtain and was not used in early house construction, there are examples of ancient dwellings marked by low mounds or banks, frequently surrounded by fosses. Examples of these have been excavated at Ballingoola, Co. Limerick, and while dating evidence was lacking—an Early Iron Age date is tentatively suggested—they

Marshland

gave good indications of the method of building a circular wooden house, presumably with wattles or other light material since there were no post-holes; outside this a deep trench was dug and the material so obtained was piled against the house walls to give them stability and added thickness. The surrounding trench not only provided this material but provided the drainage which must have been essential in such wet surroundings. Two of the houses excavated had evidently been demolished by fire—a circumstance which was fortunate from the viewpoint of excavation as the house plan and other details could be deduced from the colour-pattern on the clay surface where the burning timbers had collapsed. A third house, smaller but evidently of similar type, had not been burned and gave scant information to the excavator.

These houses conform to the construction postulated for the Manx ring-fort type of sites, but they are much smaller—about 20 feet diameter, a modest area for roofing, as against 90 feet on the Manx sites. This method of construction—clay piled against wattles or other timbers—was found also in the small hut, about 12 feet in diameter, enclosed in the Grange ring-fort (4) in the immediate vicinity of the Ballingoola houses.

One of the Ballingoola sites before excavation had a saucer-like shape, the rim being the bank caused by the collapsed house-wall. The other lacked the hollow in the middle and appeared as a low flat-topped mound, which without excavation could not be distinguished from a burial mound.

The Ballingoola sites have been dealt with at some length because they are the first of the type investigated in this country. Others not excavated are known in the same neighbourhood and comparable remains are likely to occur in other similarly marshy districts.

COASTAL DWELLING SITES

The flint-producing Mesolithic (Middle Stone Age) sites of the North-east of Ireland give the earliest evidence of a shore-dwelling tradition but, with the exception of a hearth *Kitchen-* found in a midden at Rough Island in Strangford *middens* Lough, they contain no structural remains. 'Kitchen-middens' are accumulations of ancient refuse, and they are found on various parts of the coast, particularly in regions where sandhills occur. They date from Neolithic times onward. They are generally attested by a black layer containing much charcoal in which may be found potsherds, and other antiquities, as well as scattered bones, shells, and miscellaneous debris. In these middens hearths of stone are to be noted, around which the accumulation of charcoal is more marked. Sand-dunes not covered by vegetation shift rapidly as a result of wind action and ancient middens not visible at one period may be revealed by the movement of the sand after a storm. As a result sherds, flints, and other objects are frequently not *in situ* in a layer but are found as a scatter on the surface of the sand.

The foundations of round huts—circles of boulders—have been noted on several sandhill sites, as at Whitepark Bay, Co. Antrim and at Dunfanaghy and Doagh More, *Huts and* Co. Donegal. Graves have also been found on the *graves* sandhills; these sometimes consist of little more than groups of stones, but circular settings of stones or well-constructed cists (as one at Doagh More) also occur. Observations regarding finds and structures on the sandhills have resulted mainly from collectors' activities and not much systematic work has been done on these sites, so that evidence for structures other than stone settings—of houses or graves—were not likely to be noted. Recent excavation on the Dundrum, Co. Down, sandhills not only revealed stone-built graves but showed that one had a ring-ditch around it. Post-holes and pits gave evidence of structures connected with habitation; one U-shaped group of post-holes marked the site of a hut or wind-break.

It is clear from the pottery found in some of the middens, as at Dundrum, that a number of shore-dwelling sites of this type belong to the Neolithic period. It is equally clear *Date* from other finds that habitation—probably seasonal occupation—on the sandhills continued through the Bronze and Early Iron Ages and into the Early Christian period and perhaps even into Medieval times. The Ballybunnion, Co. Kerry sandhills have produced Iron Age pins and Roman coins, while bronze pins and brooches from Co. Donegal sites give evidence of a later dating.

A somewhat different type of shore-dwelling site is the shell-mound, well known on the shores of Cork harbour. These consist of mounds of shells, mainly oysters. *Shell-* Little has been found in them beyond layers and *mounds* flecks of charcoal, and, occasionally, stones which are said to have been used for opening the shell-fish.

ANCIENT COOKING-PLACES

A type of monument found in great numbers in parts of the country and scarcely noted at all elsewhere is the ancient
cooking-place, which occurs in low-lying marshy areas
Names or near the banks of streams, and consists of a mound
of burnt stone and finely comminuted charcoal. Such
a mound is known as a *fulacht fiadh* or *fulacht fiann*. In English
they are usually referred to locally under the Anglicized forms
of these names—'fulacht fees' or 'fulacht fians' or sometimes as
'deer roasts' an interpretation of *fulacht fiadha*. Tradition
connects them with the Fianna, whose cooking-places they are
said to have been, hence the name *fulacht fiann*. They are
marked on the recent editions of the Ordnance Maps under the
title *fulacht fian*.

In their complete form these cooking-places consist of a
horseshoe-shaped mound of burnt stones, the opening towards
a stream, and excavation has shown that in the
Structure hollow of the mound is a hearth usually built of flat
stones. Outside this hearth, and between it and the
stream, is a wooden trough, which may be made of well-shaped
wooden planks, as in one near Mallow, Co. Cork. In another
at Ballinguilla, near Tullylease, Co. Cork, the sides were made
of well-fitted hazel posts and were held in position by means of
short uprights, the whole being made watertight with a clay
packing on the outside. In other cases, the trough is more
simply made from a hollowed tree-trunk.

The accepted theory regarding these cooking-places is that
the method of cooking was to heat the stones in the fire, and
then drop them into the water in the trough until
Method of this was brought to the boil. Similar cooking
cooking methods still continue among modern primitive
peoples. The mound of the fulacht fiadh is composed of the discarded stones which have become broken and
brittle from having been heated and subsequently plunged
into water, and such mounds can be recognized by the brittle
nature of the stones, usually sandstone, in them. Not all
the mounds have a horseshoe-shaped outline, but this, or

approximations to it, is most general. Others, however, may be circular or irregular in plan. They vary in size from a diameter of about 8 feet to as much as 80 feet, as in the case of one near Passage West, Co. Cork, which is an irregularly shaped mound rising to a height of about 6 feet near the centre.

These cooking-places are found frequently in the counties of Cork and Waterford, to some extent elsewhere in Munster and in the West of Ireland. They occur in the *Distribution* neighbourhood of Enniscorthy, Co. Wexford and near Rathangan, Co. Kildare. They have not been noted throughout the rest of the country. Outside Ireland they occur in parts of England and are frequent in Wales where they have attracted little notice from the archaeologists though the geologists have recorded them.

Very little work has been done to investigate these sites and what has been done has not been productive of much information, especially in the matter of datable material. *Finds* Stone axes are said to have been found in some examples in Co. Waterford. A late Bronze Age gold ornament (an expanded-ended dress fastener of the type known as a 'fibula') was found in the material of a fulacht fiadh near Balla, Co. Mayo; a flanged bronze axe (of the beginning of the Middle Bronze Age) is reported from one near Millstreet, Co. Cork, while others in the same district produced querns.

These cooking-places are mentioned by Keating in his *Forus Feasa*. He describes them as being used by the Fianna in their hunting expeditions during the summer *Literary* months (*Bealtaine* until *Samhain*) for the cooking of *references* the meat procured during the chase. In translation the passage continues: It was their custom . . . 'to dig two pits in the yellow clay of the moorland, and put some of the meat on spits to roast before the fire; and to bind another portion of it in dry bundles and set it to boil in the larger of the two pits, and keep plying them with stones that were in the fire, making them seethe often until they were cooked. And these fires were so large that their sites are to-day burnt to blackness, and these are now called Fulacht Fian by the peasantry.' Another reference in the *Agallamh Beg* in the Book of Lismore connects them with Cuchulainn, and here they are called

Fulacht na Morrigna. We find, also, other references to them but they do not give any detailed descriptions.

It would appear from the evidence of the finds and from the tradition regarding them that fulacht fiadha are another *Summary* example of a type of monument beginning in pre-historic times but continuing into the historic period.

It is possible that they are more widely distributed throughout Ireland than is at present realized and here, again, the field-worker can do useful service by noting hitherto unrecorded sites. As our knowledge of fulachta fiadha stands at present the distribution is a puzzling one—they are extremely numerous in South Munster, rare in some other districts, and not known to exist elsewhere.

While these pages were in proof a report came in of the excavation of a *fulacht fiadh* near Ballyvourney, Co. Cork. For *Ballyvourney* the first time one of these sites was completely *site* excavated and revealed two hearths, a wood-lined pit for boiling, a stone-lined pit for roasting and a wigwam-like structure evidently intended for storing the meat (41, 42). Experiment showed that the cooking of the meat (both roasting and boiling) could be carried out quite efficiently with heated stones—the wooden trough contained one hundred gallons of water, which was brought to the boil in half-an-hour. The site yielded no dating evidence.

CRANNÓGS

A *crannóg* is an ancient Irish lake dwelling. The name from *crann*, a tree, is due to the large amount of timber used in the construction of most of these sites. Lake dwellings *Definition* are known from various parts of the world and from different times down to the present day. They differ in the manner of construction; some are pile dwellings, the houses being raised on piles driven into the lake bottom; others are built on foundations of logs, stones, or other materials on marshes or lake shores. The Irish crannóg is an artificially constructed island on which the house or houses of the crannóg-dwellers were built.

The use of island dwellings in Ireland is well attested historically and some of the sites mentioned are referred to as *crannógs* in the annals and in other historical documents. The word was introduced into archaeological literature and the crannóg as a type was brought to notice over a century ago when Petrie and Wilde investigated the site at Lagore, near Dunshaughlin, Co. Meath in 1839, their attention having been drawn to it by the finds of antiquities made there by men digging for bones. The Lagore crannóg has recently (1934–6) been excavated completely.

The site of a crannóg presents varying appearances at the present day. It may still be an island in a lake, but in many cases it is distinguishable as a mound in a bog. *Appearance* Such a mound, when investigated, will be found *and* to have been built when the local conditions were *discovery* different—the surrounding area having at that time been either open water or so marshy as to make the site very difficult of access. In many cases crannógs have been revealed by the drainage or partial drainage of lakes. Numbers of those recorded in the archaeological literature of the last century came to notice because of the drainage programme then carried out, and others have been revealed recently by the lowering of lake and river levels. On the other hand, there are instances of low islands, possibly crannógs, which have disappeared because of the partial drainage of the

30   MOTTE ON RING-FORT, KNOCKAHOLET, CO. ANTRIM

31   GIANT'S RING DOLMEN, CO. DOWN—SURROUNDING BANK BEHIND

32 SOUTERRAIN AT BALLYCATTEEN, CO. CORK

33 SOUTERRAIN TUNNEL, DUNBEG, CO. KERRY

34 RECTANGULAR NEOLITHIC HOUSE, KNOCKADOON, LOUGH GUR, CO. LIMERICK

35 HUT ON COAD MOUNTAIN, CO. KERRY

36   STONE HOUSE AT BALLYVOURNEY, CO. CORK—AFTER EXCAVATION

37   ROUND HUT AT THE "SPECTACLES", LOUGH GUR—DURING
EXCAVATION

38   PAIR OF CONJOINED CLOCHÁNS, DINGLE PENINSULA, CO. KERRY

39   MODERN FARM OUT-BUILDINGS ROOFED WITH STONE, DINGLE PENINSULA

40 MEDIEVAL HOUSES, CAHERGUILLAMORE, CO. LIMERICK—DURING EXCAVATION

41 *Fulacht fiadh* AT BALLYVOURNEY, CO. CORK—BEFORE EXCAVATION

42 *Fulacht fiadh* AT BALLYVOURNEY, CO. CORK—DURING EXCAVATION
(FRAMEWORK OF HUT RECONSTRUCTED)

43 BALLINDERRY 2 CRANNÓG, CO. OFFALY—DURING EXCAVATION

44 DOLMEN AT PROLEEK,
CO. LOUTH

45 WEDGE-SHAPED
GALLERY GRAVE,
PROLEEK, CO. LOUTH

46 COURT CAIRN DEERPARK, CO. SLIGO

47 COURT CAIRN CREEVYKEEL, CO. SLIGO—DURING EXCAVATION

48   WEDGE-SHAPED GALLERY GRAVE, POULAPHUCA, CO. CLARE

49   WEDGE-SHAPED GALLERY GRAVE, PARKNABINNIA, CO. CLARE

50   DOLMEN AT BROWNE'S HILL, CO. CARLOW

51   WEDGE-SHAPED GALLERY GRAVE, ALTAR, CO. CORK

52   CAIRN ON SEEFIN MOUNTAIN, CO. WICKLOW

53   ENTRANCE TO PASSAGE-GRAVE IN SEEFIN CAIRN

54 CAIRNS S AND T, LOUGHCREW, CO. MEATH

55 CAIRN S, LOUGHCREW, CO. MEATH

56 NEWGRANGE, CO. MEATH, SHOWING SOME OF ENCIRCLING STANDING STONES

57 TUMULUS NEAR NEWGRANGE, BOYNE VALLEY

58 NEWGRANGE: DECORATED STONE AT ENTRANCE

lakes in which they stood. In these cases the lowering of the water level caused drying and hence the shrinkage of the material composing the island, while the growth of vegetation around it caused it to merge into the surrounding area.

The builders of a crannóg, having selected their site, made the island by laying down layers of various materials, of which peat and brushwood were the most usual, though *Construction* logs, stones, straw, rushes, bracken, and animal bones were also used. Pointed timbers were driven in at the edge of the island to form a protective palisade; others placed in haphazard fashion served to consolidate the layers of material (43).

Crannógs vary considerably in structure—due to different methods of building and also because of changes made during occupation, which sometimes extended over a long period. In many cases the evidence is incomplete because the sites were not fully investigated or because they had been seriously disturbed before they were investigated. Three large crannógs have been excavated in recent times—Lagore and the two sites in Ballinderry Lough on the Westmeath-Offaly border— and of these Ballinderry No. 1 (Westmeath) gave the most complete data as to its original construction and subsequent changes. This site appears to be typical of many others where information is less complete and it is, therefore, worth while to summarize the details regarding its structure.

The first stage of the building at Ballinderry No. 1 (in the latter part of the tenth century) was to place in position a platform of timbers about 20 feet square. Similar *Ballinderry* foundation platforms had already been noted on *No. 1* other crannógs and it was thought that they were made as rafts and floated over the site where the crannóg was to be built. At Ballinderry this had not been done because there was no sign that the logs had been fastened together. They were held in position by pegs driven into the lake bottom, indicating that the lake level was low when the platform was built. Around the platform and about 10 feet from it, an irregular circle was marked out with light stakes. Within this small timbers were laid down, some radially and some at right angles to these. The timbers had evidently been taken from an earlier building because many of them were

D

worked; and some gave evidence of highly developed carpentry. Over the platform and the surrounding timbers, layers of peat alternating with thin layers of brushwood were laid down; in these layers animal bones occurred frequently. Here and there the builders placed flat stones to consolidate the peat and brushwood. On this deposit timbers were placed in considerable quantity to form the foundation for a house floor, the floor itself being of carefully woven wickerwork. The timbers forming the foundation for the house floor covered a horseshoe-shaped area about 52 feet across at its widest part. The open space in the centre contained the hearth; an irregular spread of ashes indicated that the fire was moved from time to time. Around the house and forming a strong fence at the edge of the island was a palisade of piles which enclosed an area 85 feet in greatest diameter. The palisade varied in strength and in general was strongest on the side where the island could be more easily approached from the land. Here as many as ten rows of piles formed the palisade. On the opposite side of the island the palisade was lighter, but scattered piles outside it appear to have been intended as an obstacle against boats. The entrance was marked by a gap in the palisade and was approached by a causeway made of a brushwood layer and protected by a row of posts on either side. The entrance and causeway gave evidence that the crannóg could be reached on foot—at least during the dry seasons. Provision was also made for boats to reach the crannóg by building a quay on the side opposite the entrance. The quay was made by laying down horizontal timbers and covering these with peat; it appears to have been a late feature of the site.

The original house on the crannóg was abandoned probably because of the sinking of its floor due to the unsatisfactory nature of the foundations. The surface was then raised by the use of material similar to that employed in the foundation layers, but with the addition now of layers of gravel. Included in the fill was a discarded dug-out boat. Upon the new surface two houses were built, not centrally as in the case of the original house but near the edge of the crannóg, around the greater portion of which a new palisade was built—this time of squared planks. When the two secondary houses were abandoned a layer of white clay mixed with grasses was laid down and on

this a fourth house, of which only scanty remains were recovered, was built. Finally, coins of Elizabeth and James II
found in the superficial layer gave evidence of a transitory
occupation at a late date.

Many of the features noted at Ballinderry No. 1 appear, on
the present evidence, to be typical of the large crannógs of Early
Other sites Christian times. Parallels can be found for the
method of building, the materials used, the palisade
and enclosed house and for the changes in structure
and the late continuity of occupation. At Lagore three palisades,
representing successive occupation phases, were found. Scattered piles occurred outside the palisade—as also, though less
profusely, at Ballinderry No. 2—and it is suggested that these
gave added protection in the manner of the *chevaux de frise*
of the stone forts. Nineteenth-century descriptions of the
Lagore site indicate a system of elaborate cubicle-like structures
connected with the latest palisade, which was built of planks,
but the excavation did not give confirmation of these structures.
The plank palisade at Lagore was, in any case, a carefully
constructed feature. Slotted uprights held horizontal planks in
position so as to form a continuous wooden wall around the site.

There is no indication that any crannóg held a large number
of houses. All the evidence points to the fact that these sites
Homesteads were single homesteads and not villages. We may
suppose that the inhabitants consisted of one
family together with their servants, among whom
might be included tradesmen of various classes; evidence of
metal- and glass-working as well as less specialized occupations
has been found on crannógs. In the manner of its occupation
the Irish crannóg differs sharply from the English lake village,
such as those at Glastonbury and Meare in Somerset. The
Somerset sites contained a number of houses surrounded by a
palisade; they resemble the Irish crannóg because of their
geographical environment but are clearly different in the
social organization which gave rise to them.

Published lists of crannógs in Ireland enumerate somewhat
over two hundred and twenty examples. The number has
since been augmented by the discovery of many sites and there
are presumably a great number yet awaiting discovery. Even
if we make allowance for such an augmentation of the list

of crannógs we must still conclude that they are not nearly so numerous as are forts in this country, and their distribution is much more restricted. They are found most *Distribution* frequently in the area west and north-west of the central plain, but are known also outside this region, while Co. Antrim, well away from the main area of distribution, has a large number of crannógs. Apart from the accidents of discovery, which depend largely on the number of interested workers in the different areas (a factor which must always influence distributional studies) the concentration of crannógs in certain districts is probably due to the existence in these districts of lakes inviting to the crannóg builders.

The dating of crannógs covers a range as long as, or even longer, than that of the forts. The varied assemblage of relics from Irish lake dwellings as seen in museums had given *Dating* evidence of this even before recent systematic excavation provided confirmation and, indeed, showed a hitherto unsuspected antiquity for crannóg building. Three recently excavated crannógs have been shown to date from comparatively late in Early Christian times: Ballinderry No. 1, Co. Westmeath was built in the latter part of the tenth century; habitation continued into the eleventh century while intermittent occupation seems to have continued until the seventeenth century. Ballinderry No. 2, Co. Offaly, a site slightly over a mile from Ballinderry No. 1, belongs to the end of the sixth and the early seventh century. Lagore, a royal residence, was built about the middle of the seventh century and continued in occupation until the tenth. A recently excavated crannóg at Lough Faughan, Co. Down, was occupied in Early Christian times and in the thirteenth century—whether continuously or not is uncertain.

Under the Early Christian site at Ballinderry was a habitation stratum dating to a late stage in the Late Bronze Age with which was associated a wooden building and a number of small wicker structures. The wooden building was of peculiar construction. Planks with perforations to take uprights were laid on the ground in such an arrangement that they formed an approximately square house (35 feet side) divided into seven long narrow bays. The house was surrounded by piles which either gave it protection or served to hold a projecting roof; two lines of piles marked the approach to the house. The wicker structures were circular buildings of very small diameter (about three to seven feet) and it is suggested that they were used as granaries. The house and the wicker huts were placed directly on ground level (the huts sunken in the ground) and must have been built when the lake level was low. They represented an island settlement rather than a true crannóg, but before the settlement was abandoned a portion of the surface had been raised by layers of brushwood and stones—placed over some of the wicker huts.

Of similar Late Bronze Age (or transition to Iron Age) date was a true crannóg investigated at Knocknalappa, Co. Clare. This site yielded bronzes of Late Bronze Age type and pottery that showed Early Iron Age affinities—similar to pottery from habitation sites in the south of England. Two islands in the North—Rough Island in Lough Enagh, Co. Derry and Island MacHugh, Co. Tyrone—were settled in Neolithic times, but there is no definite indication in either case of artificial island construction at that early date. At Island MacHugh the Bronze Age people laid down wooden floors for their dwellings and, perhaps, placed some brushwood at the island edge.

A site which can more properly be regarded as a crannóg of early date was excavated at Rathjordan, Co. Limerick, where an artificial island was made by laying down a stone layer over a foundation of peat, brushwood, and timbers. The island was small, the foundation layer being about eleven metres and the stone layer eight metres in diameter, and it must have been used for some short-term activity and not for lengthy occupation. A fragment of Beaker pottery found in a hearth over the crannóg shows that the date of the crannóg cannot be later than Early Bronze Age times.

Chance finds or finds made by collectors, who in some cases ransacked crannóg sites—prolific sources of antiquities—also
Chance gave evidence of the long duration of the crannóg type
finds of settlement. A famous crannóg was that at Lisna-crogher, Co. Antrim; because of the splendid material it produced, including the fine ornamented scabbards of Iron Age date, it is unfortunate that it did not receive better treatment than that given it by the relic-seeking collectors. Crannógs dating from the early centuries of the Christian era

are Moylarg, Co. Antrim and Ardakillin, Co. Roscommon. Bronze Age finds have also been noted from crannógs. It was usual to explain these away by suggesting that they were introduced accidentally in the structural material but, in view of the now established Bronze Age dating of some crannógs, such an explanation is not necessary in all cases. The main bulk of the museum material from Irish crannógs does, however, belong to Early Christian times and it seems clear that, however early their origin, the majority and also the largest examples are Early Christian in date.

The introduction of the practice of crannóg building into Ireland is still a matter of conjecture, but that the beginnings were early must be maintained in view of the *Development* recently excavated early examples which have *of crannógs* been mentioned. The first European lake dwellings arose as a result of the fusion of the Mesolithic (Middle Stone Age) tradition of moor or lakeside settlements with the new culture of the Neolithic. In Ireland—as also in Britain (at Ehenside Tarn in Cumberland)—the Neolithic brought the same tradition of lake settlements. The Rathjordan crannóg is a true crannóg in structure, but its small size and brief period of use suggest that it grew out of special local needs—similar to those which caused the building of the stone hearths (also with Beaker pottery) in the neighbouring bog at Rockbarton. Crannóg building in the Late Bronze Age is testified by Knocknalappa and in the Early Iron Age by Lisnacrogher, and subsequently by numerous examples. It is possible that crannóg building was given a fresh impetus at more than one period—due to new incursions and to social conditions—but the large numbers of lake dwellings which we possess are the results of the continuance of an early tradition in a favourable environment in lakes and marshes.

The term 'crannóg' and our stressing of the use of timber in the building of these sites should not obscure the fact that stone was also used to a considerable extent in certain *Stone as* examples, for instance in many of the Co. Cavan *material* crannógs. We have already noted the use of stone as packing, together with peat, brushwood, and other materials. Stone was sometimes put in to form a breakwater on one side of the island or around the piles to keep them secure against the wash of the water. The Lough Faughan, Co. Down, crannóg was surrounded by a stone kerb and stone forms the foundation and the surround at Bolin Island, Lough Gur. Some examples are made very largely by piling up stones and may be encircled by well-built stone walls—as the well-known example in the lake near Fair Head, Co. Antrim and those in some of the Connemara lakes. The dividing line between a true crannóg and an island fort becomes rather difficult in these cases, especially when a stone fort is erected on an island which is in part artificially constructed.

From the viewpoint of the excavator crannógs have an especial importance not possessed by other sites. The moisture which is usual on a crannóg tends to preserve *Preservation* objects which would completely decay under *of objects* drier conditions. Thus the finds from a crannóg often include articles of wood, leather, and textiles, and so they give a more complete picture of the everyday life of the inhabitants than is available when all organic materials have disappeared. Apart from the objects found, the evidence from crannógs goes to demonstrate that carpentry of good quality was practised in ancient times—even at an early date. We have already noted the worked timbers of the Late Bronze Age stratum at Ballinderry No. 2 and also the foundation timbers of Ballinderry No. 1 which are, as the excavator remarks, 'good evidence for the high development of the carpenter's craft in Ireland by the Viking Age'.

The peculiar nature of the crannóg sites and their isolation from farmland directs attention to the type of economy followed by the inhabitants. It has been found that a *Economy* considerable portion of the food must have been provided by domestic animals of which the bones are found in large quantities on and around the sites. Agriculture was also practised, as is shown by the querns and the agricultural implements found. It would appear that the inhabitants of the crannógs were farmers whose land was presumably on the neighbouring shores of the lakes on which their dwellings were built. Small-scale industries, such as metal-working, were also carried on as is shown by crucibles and slag found on the sites. To reach the dwellings, causeways may sometimes have been built, but in other cases boats must have been used and these boats—hollowed tree-trunks—were found in some of the excavated crannógs. We have noted the existence of a boat-slip at Ballinderry No. 1; one was found also at Knocknalappa.

In general, the crannógs were the equivalent of the ring-forts, though built on lakes and marshes instead of on dry land. They afforded a measure of protection, and the economy of life of the inhabitants was similar to that of the fort dwellers. In Ireland they did not hold village communities, as did the site at Glastonbury in England, but were similar to the smaller forts in being homesteads of single families depending on agriculture and stock-raising as the main sources of subsistence.

Structures of wood and hearths of stone are frequently found in bogs but are not necessarily connected with crannógs.

Other structures in bogs   A wooden hut built in two low stories like the bunks on a ship was revealed as a result of turf-cutting at Drumkelin, Inver, Co. Donegal. A stone axe found in the hut is thought to have been used in its construction. Somewhat similar huts, but of only one story, were found at Kilnamaddoo, Co. Fermanagh. These huts may have been used for storage—butter wrapped in cow-hide was found in one of them. The Drumkelin hut, built on a foundation of sea-sand, was surrounded by a stockade and the site is therefore sometimes described as a crannóg, but this is hardly warranted. At Cargaghoge, Co. Monaghan, a

Wooden houses   wooden house floor about eighteen feet square with central stone hearth and approach causeway built of timbers was found under deep peat and supported on hazel and birch branches. These and other descriptions of houses and other structures in bogs are fairly frequent in the archaeological literature but the indications of date are in most cases meagre and indefinite.

Palings of stakes (usually of birch) are found now and again in the course of turf-cutting, but since only a small portion is

Palings and roads   uncovered at one time, sufficient attention has not been given them to determine their lay-out and function. They may represent enclosures on the marshy surface prior to the formation of the upper layers of peat. Roads built of logs, sometimes elaborately built, are frequently discovered in bogs; they may be of various dates but the association of a bronze spear-head with one in the Bog of Allen demonstrates that such a roadway may be as old as the Bronze Age.

Hearths due to temporary occupation of ancient marsh areas have also been found in bogs. The technique of pollen-analysis (the determination of climatic sequences *Hearths* from the percentages of the various types of tree pollen) has corroborated the dating given by a study of the pottery (Early Bronze Age) found in some of these hearths at Rockbarton, Co. Limerick. In the case of the older discoveries (for instance, some of the houses in bogs), it is sometimes tantalizing to read that 'some pieces of very rude pottery' were found, there being no attempt to illustrate this material, which is most valuable as an indication of date. Even yet there is little doubt that structures are found in the course of turf-cutting and are not brought to scientific notice, though finds of objects are much more readily reported. The remedy for this must be in the keenness of the local observer who is willing to watch for such discoveries and note them with sufficient fullness and accuracy.

MEGALITHIC TOMBS

During the centuries towards the end of the third millennium B.C., there spread throughout the Mediterranean area, along the Atlantic coasts of Europe, northwards into Scandinavia and the North European mainland the custom of building great tombs of stone intended for what is known as 'collective burial', that is to say each tomb contained many burials. The distribution outlined does not cover all the area in which such tombs are known, for they are found also in parts of Africa and Asia, but we are concerned only with that movement which brought them to Ireland.

Origin and spread
The origin of the custom of building these tombs need not be discussed here since its discussion would lead us far afield and we would not find unanimity of opinion regarding it among archaeologists. It must suffice to say that the cult arose in the Mediterranean area and came to this country by two main routes, the one from the Iberian Peninsula, with, perhaps, Brittany as a point of contact *en route*, the other, at present less well defined, overland across France.

Names
To these tombs is applied the name 'megalithic' (from Greek *megas*, great, and *lithos*, stone) because they are, in so many cases, constructed of large stones. As a descriptive title, however, the name does not cover all classes of megalithic tombs, since some of them are built, not of great stones, but of small slabs in the form of a dry-stone walling, while others that belong to the same cultural heritage are cut partly or entirely in rock. The term 'megalithic' continues to be used for this whole family of tombs because it has long-standing currency in the archaeological literature in many European languages. It has the further advantage that it lends itself to use as an adjective in such contexts as 'megalithic religion', 'megalithic colonization', 'megalithic period'. 'Rude stone monuments', which was used formerly is not superior as a descriptive expression and cannot conveniently be used adjectivally. This latter objection applies also to 'Chambered tombs', which has come into use in Britain;

apart from this it is simple and is excellent as a descriptive term, since these structures consist essentially of a burial chamber, covered in most cases by a mound of earth or stones.

Popularly the tombs are known under various terms. The word *cromlech* which will be found on the earlier editions of the Ordnance Maps and in the older archaeological literature has now fallen completely into disfavour because in Brittany, from whence the word comes, it designates not a tomb but a stone circle. Its place was taken by another name of Celtic origin— *dolmen*—but this is now usually confined to certain simpler types of chambered tombs. Names used for megalithic tombs in different districts of Ireland include *giant's grave*, *Leaba Dhiarmuda's Gráinne, cloghogle;* some individual tombs have special names as Leaba Chaillighe, Leaba na Muice and so on. Terms such as *druids' altar* or *druids' table* have been foisted on the popular nomenclature by the speculations of earlier antiquaries and have nothing to recommend them, either as traditional or descriptive titles, since these burial places had nothing to do with the druids nor were they intended either as altars or tables.

There are at least a thousand chambered tombs extant in Ireland; countless others have been destroyed in the course of

Number time, the stones of which they were built having been robbed for various purposes. In spite of much recent work—and few problems in archaeology attract such attention as do the megalithic tombs—the total number of such structures is not accurately known; some still remain unrecorded and, in the absence of detailed surveys, the typology of many known examples is yet unclear. Indeed, in numerous cases it must remain undefined because too much of the tomb structure has been removed to allow of certainty as to the complete form. It should also be remembered when we look at a megalith that we are often looking at the skeleton of the tomb only, the covering mound and the subsidiary features having been removed. Thus we may see the chamber, consisting of supporting stones and roof, when the cairn of stones which once hid it has gone; or the ground plan alone may be recognizable when uprights only remain after cairn and roofing material have vanished. Incomplete tombs, or even relatively small portions of tombs may often be ascribed with confidence to their respective types in a classification which is based on a study of more complete specimens, or on knowledge gained collectively from numbers of examples.

In general megalithic tombs belong to two main groups—gallery graves and passage-graves—which are distinct in their architecture and in their cultural affinities. This broad *Types* twofold division allows of subdivision into classes which are in part due to devolution from primary types, and in part to important distinctions of origin and to colonization by different groups of megalithic builders. We shall deal with gallery graves first because on present evidence one of the sub-types of this group (the court cairn) is earliest in the Irish series. The gallery grave, as the name implies, is characterized by a long narrow chamber in which the burials are placed. Variations in ground plan and other features enable us to subdivide gallery graves into a threefold classification; court cairns, southern wedge-shaped galleries, and northern wedge-shaped galleries.

The name 'court cairn' is one that has recently come into use to designate gallery graves that incorporate in their structure a ritual unroofed court (Fig. 3). The name has the advan-*Court* tage of stressing a feature which occurs in the tombs *cairns* commonly known as 'horned cairns' and also in the variant for which the name 'lobster-claw cairns' was coined, thus emphasizing the essential unity of the whole class. In the horned cairns the ritual area is in the form of an approximately semicircular forecourt, placed at one end of the cairn and marked by uprights forming a façade through the middle of which access was gained to the gallery. In the lobster-claw cairns (which we may now call 'full-court cairns') the uprights enclose an oval or circular area from which access was gained to one or to several galleries. Variants may occur on the simpler theme of the fore-court cairn or on the more elaborate full-court type. Thus instead of a single forecourt as at Browndod, Co. Antrim, one finds examples with forecourt at each end as at Cohaw, Co. Cavan. In the Cohaw tomb the galleries lie along the long axis of the cairn and at the middle a closed chamber forms the junction between them. At Ballybriest, Co. Derry, the two galleries to which the dual forecourts give access are unconnected features not on the same axis.

BROWNDOD, CO. ANTRIM

CLADY HALLIDAY, CO. TYRONE

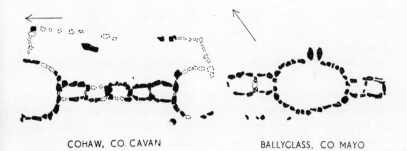

COHAW, CO. CAVAN

BALLYGLASS, CO. MAYO

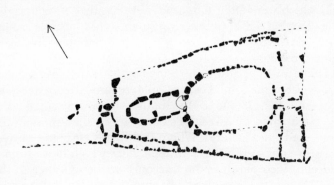

CREEVYKEEL, CO. SLIGO

0   10   20   30   40   50   60 feet

FIG. 3.   Court cairns

Browndod and Clady Halliday: forecourt type; Cohaw: double
forecourt; Ballyglass and Creevykeel: full-court.

The type of full-court cairn with oval court, at one end of which is an entrance, at the other the gallery, is well exemplified in the monument excavated at Creevykeel, Co. *Full-court* Sligo (47). An elaboration on this theme occurs at *cairns* Ballybeg, Co. Mayo, where a semicircular forecourt gives access to the oval court. Examples with the entrance on the long side of the oval court occur at Deerpark, Co. Sligo and at Ballyglass, Co. Mayo; in the latter there is a gallery at either end of the court; in the former there is a single gallery at one end and there are two at the other.

The monument mentioned at Deerpark, near Sligo (46), was formerly a subject of much speculation. Known under the name of 'Leact Chon Mhic Ruis', it has been called 'the Irish Stonehenge' because the uprights forming the entrance to the galleries have the lintels in position upon them and these features brought to mind the trilithons of the famous but quite different monument in England. The recognition that the Deerpark megalith represents a burial monument of the court cairn type solved a problem and placed it in its true context with other tombs of this class. The galleries in these tombs are divided into segments by pairs of uprights (jambs) between which are frequently set low stones forming sills. Roofing is by lintels which were often supported not directly on the uprights of the chamber walls, but on projecting stones (corbels) which slightly narrowed the space to be spanned and gave increased height to the roof.

It is not always possible to recognize the outline of the cairn which covered the tomb because collapse and interference have so often obscured its limits. It was normally de-*Cairn* marcated by a kerb of stones—lower than those in the *outline* court and gallery. Where the plan is clear the cairn is usually seen to have straight sides which taper from a broad end, incorporating the forecourt or the entrance to the oval full court, to a narrow end behind the gallery. In the dual forecourt type the cairn plan is approximately rectangular.

The distribution of court cairns in Ireland is almost entirely confined to the northern part of the country—north of the central plain. In the eastern part of the court cairn area the simpler forecourt type is found, while the elaborate full-court examples occur mainly in the west—in Sligo, Mayo, and south Donegal (Cloughanmore in Glencolumbkille). Two theories have been put forward to explain the distribution pattern. One is that the builders entered the *Distribution* country in the neighbourhood of Carlingford Lough and that in the movement westward more elaborate tomb forms developed. The other theory postulates an entry in the west, possibly in the neighbourhood of Killala Bay, Co. Mayo, where there is a concentration of full-court cairns, and argues a simplification of the tomb type in the course of an eastward expansion.

Excavation has produced evidence of a Neolithic date for the court cairns. They have yielded leaf-shaped flint arrow-heads and round-bottomed shouldered bowls of hard smooth *Date* ware related to the 'Windmill Hill' fabrics found in Britain. A number of forecourt cairns (including dual forecourt examples) have been investigated in Ulster, and one full-court monument (Creevykeel) in the west. The dating evidence at Creevykeel is parallel to that from the simpler structures so that the chronological data available do not warrant a judgement between the theory of east-west evolution or that of west-east devolution. While burial in some court cairns continued into the Bronze Age, they, alone of Irish megalithic tomb types, present coherent evidence for a Neolithic dating and, pending further excavation, we can only say that examples of both the simpler and the more complex types were built in Neolithic times.

It may be accepted that the ritual court, which is the distinguishing feature of these tombs, was used for burial ceremonial, though we have no means of knowing the *Origin* exact nature of the rites practised. Varying expressions of the forecourt idea are found in the long cairns of South Wales and West England (the 'Cotswold-Severn' group), in English long barrows with crescentic wooden façades, in Scottish 'horned-cairns', and in the so-called 'giants' tombs' of Sardinia. The full court recalls the Neolithic temples of Malta and the stone settings (sometimes circular) in front of some of the Iberian passage graves. All these give indications of possible relationships; the monuments in Britain may be derived from the same source as the Irish examples, though it is possible that the Scottish ones have an Irish ancestry. The ultimate origin must be to the south, though none of the types found in the Mediterranean, the Iberian peninsula, or in France can be convincingly shown to be prototypes. They may only have provided an inspiration which gave rise to a specialized Irish development.

The tombs which we have called wedge-shaped galleries (Fig. 4) are simpler in structure than the court cairns and of the two varieties—northern and southern—the latter is in *Gallery* general simpler than the former. It is also more *graves* numerous. There are probably as many as three or four hundred wedge-shaped gallery tombs in the country of which total about two-thirds are of the southern variety. In the more complete and fully developed examples the distinction between the northern and southern galleries is clear, but in many cases too little remains of the structure to allow of certainty as to type and in other cases the features suggest an interplay between the two classes. On the whole, however, the distribution and the typology combine to distinguish these two separate gallery-grave classes which may have a common origin and which must have cultural relationships.

The southern wedge-shaped gallery consists in the majority of cases of a long chamber, broader and higher at one end (51). The chamber sides (and sometimes the end) are *Southern* usually built of a double line of slabs. It has been *'wedges'* suggested that this 'double walling' was due to the nature of the building material; thin slabs of shale or sandstone, when used in a double row with a stone filling between would give stability to the monument. On the other hand, the outer row of uprights was so placed as to provide little, if any, support for the roof and evidently represents a traditional architectural feature. The roof is made of flat slabs. The tombs in Co. Clare are sometimes roofed with a single large limestone slab—obtained from the local rock—and the sides are also constructed of similar large slabs frequently not doubled (48). This leads to a neatness of construction which has caused these structures to be described as simple 'box-like' graves; in fact, however, they possess features (wedge-shaped ground plan and sloping roof) which place them in the general group of southern galleries (49).

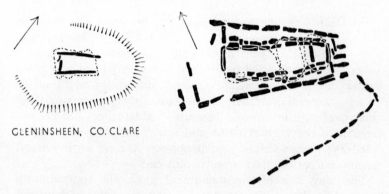

GLENINSHEEN, CO. CLARE

LABBACALLEE, CO. CORK

BALLYEDMONDUFF, CO. DUBLIN

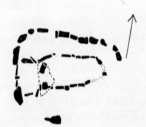

LOUGHASH, CO. TYRONE

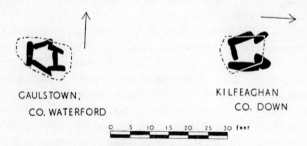

GAULSTOWN,
CO. WATERFORD

KILFEAGHAN
CO. DOWN

0   5   10   15   20   25   30 feet

FIG. 4. Gallery graves

Gleninsheen and Labbacallee: southern 'wedges'; Ballyedmonduff
and Loughash: northern 'wedges'; Gaulstown and Kilfeaghan:
portal dolmens.

The cairn outline around these tombs is not always clear. A kerb either never existed or is not any longer in evidence; *Cairn outline* again the stones of the cairn may have been removed or, on the other hand, field stones may have been piled around the monument. Such observation as is possible shows the tombs to have had in most cases a cairn of short oval outline. In one instance—Labbacallee, Co. Cork—portion of the kerb remains and shows that it was straight-sided and wedge-shaped and it appears to have an in-curved termination at the narrower, eastern end.

The long axis of the monument generally approximates (with wide deviations) to an east-west line, the higher and wider end being towards the west.

While most of the tombs are single-chambered, a few have a second, smaller chamber at the eastern end of the structure. *'Port-hole'* Since this feature occurs in the most notable (the most elaborate and greatest) of all these tombs, that at Labbacallee, Co. Cork, it has erroneously been regarded as of much more general occurrence than is in fact the case. The dividing slab which separates the large from the small chamber at Labbacallee has one of the upper corners broken away, leaving a roughly curved outline. This appears to be a deliberate removal of the corner and since the same feature occurs in one of the other two-chambered tombs (Deerpark, Co. Clare) it is taken to be a parallel to the circular 'port-hole' which is found in several megalithic areas abroad. The port-hole is a ritual feature interpreted as an opening for the passage of the soul of the dead. In a complete form it is very rare in Ireland.

In the gallery grave at Lough Gur and in some of those in the neighbourhood of Rear Cross, Co. Tipperary, a small chamber occurs at the western end. This may be related to the occurrence of an ante-chamber or portico found in the northern wedge-shaped galleries, to be described presently.

The name 'southern wedge-shaped gallery' suggests the southern distribution. In fact, however, their centre of density *Distribution* lies to the south-west. They are frequent in Cork and Kerry. They occur in eastern Limerick and western Tipperary and are numerous in Co. Clare, especially on the limestone area of the Burren. Some are found in southern Galway and also on the Aran Islands, which are geographically an extension of Co. Clare, a fact which accounts for the similarity of the Aran tombs to those on the Burren limestone.

The northern wedge-shaped gallery differs from the southern type in that the western end-stone of the main chamber is set back from the flat façade of the tomb so as to form a *Northern* portico. The chamber sides and 'double walling' *'wedges'* may be almost parallel or more distinctly converging to give a wedge-shaped plan, and the cairn tends to have a rounded, horseshoe-form eastern end. The roof is formed of large slabs sometimes supported on corbels. An example frequently quoted as a type-specimen of this class is the tomb at Dunteige, Co. Antrim and another, well to the south, is that at Moylisha, Co. Wicklow. At Ballyedmonduff, Co. Dublin, there is a multiple walling of uprights and a clearly defined kerb. This site proved on excavation to have, in addition to portico and long gallery normal to the type, a small closed chamber at the eastern end. A further peculiarity of this tomb is the occurrence of two small uprights in the small chamber; these did not support the roof or serve other structural function and may be related to the jambs in the court cairns.

The northern gallery graves are found in Ulster generally except in the counties of Down and Armagh, they occur in the west, mainly in the Sligo-Leitrim area, and there is a scatter along the east of the country (45) southward to Co. Wicklow.

Of the southern wedge class only two examples have been excavated—Labbacallee and Lough Gur. Of the northern type the following have been excavated—Kilhoyle and *Date* Boviel, Co. Derry, Loughash (two sites) and Clogherny, Co. Tyrone, Ballyedmonduff, Co. Dublin and Moylisha, Co. Wicklow. In general the dating evidence has been consistent for both types; the occurrences of Beaker pottery in several examples indicates a date in Early Bronze Age times with evidence of survival of use to a later period in some instances. The similarity of the two types of gallery grave and the fact that they have produced the same dating material suggests their relationship and their possible derivation from a common source. Their different distributions seem to indicate separate introductions into the country—possibly from France, where gallery type megaliths are well represented. A coarse type of pottery (formerly misinterpreted as Late Bronze Age urn fragments) occurs in some of these tombs. It has been found in profusion on habitation sites (Neolithic to Middle Bronze Age) in the Lough Gur neighbourhood and its general similarity to pottery found in the galleries of the Seine basin strengthens the suggestion of French origin of the Irish galleries.

While the number of Irish passage-graves (probably between one hundred and fifty and two hundred) is smaller than the total of the gallery-grave class, there are included *Passage-* among them much more spectacular monuments and *graves* very important groups. Indeed certain examples of this class must be placed with the greatest known prehistoric remains—great structures which bear witness to the prestige of the leaders of the communities that built them and indicate the high degree of social organization of these communities.

Essentially a passage-grave consists of a burial chamber which is entered by a long narrow passage (52, 53), the whole being covered by a round mound usually surrounded by a *Plan* kerb (45). In its simplest form the chamber is circular, as at Tibradden, Co. Dublin, but other ground plans are achieved by the provision of cells opening off the central chamber. One of the tombs in the Dowth Mound on the Boyne has one side chamber. The more famous neighbouring mound at Newgrange has three—two side chambers and an end chamber, thus giving the cruciform plan which occurs in so many Irish passage-graves and which, if not an Irish originality, is a standardization of tendencies already in evidence in Iberia.

Further complexity of plan (Fig. 5) is introduced by the provision around the central chamber area of a large number of cells—as in some of the tombs at Loughcrew, Co. Meath and Carrowkeel, Co. Sligo. At both these places and also at Dowth and elsewhere the passage is divided into segments and the central chamber is separated from the cells by means of 'septal stones' or sills reminiscent of those used to segment the galleries of the court cairns.

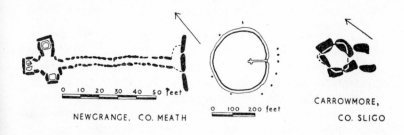

NEWGRANGE, CO. MEATH

CARROWMORE, CO. SLIGO

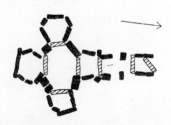

CARROWKEEL (K), CO. SLIGO

CARROWKEEL (F), CO. SLIGO

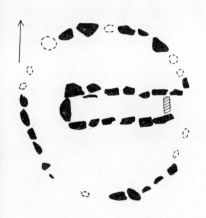

HARRISTOWN, CO. WATERFORD

BALTINGLASS, CO. WICKLOW

FIG. 5. Passage-graves

Newgrange and Carrowkeel (K): cruciform plan; Carrowkeel (F):
multiple cells; Baltinglass: simple type of chamber; Carrowmore:
'B-dolmen'; Harristown: V-shaped passage-grave.

The passage, being narrow, was roofed in a simple manner with lintels but the chamber was usually roofed in a dome fashion by corbelling—a technique already referred to in connexion with souterrains and clocháns. While the corbelling was sometimes built of small stones (Tibradden) it was generally of large slabs and, when the roofs have remained in position, they are impressive pieces of construction. The excellence of the work and the height—rising to nearly 20 feet above the ground—makes the Newgrange roof one of the most impressive features of this great monument (59). The corbelling of the centre chamber and the lintels of the passage in Newgrange are supported on dry-stone masonry, in front of which are upright stones which give no support to the roof but serve to hold firm the dry-stone walling and the cairn material behind and also serve to provide suitable flat surfaces for the carvings which are a feature of this and of so many of these tombs.

Corbelled roof

An important aspect of the distribution of passage-graves is the fact that there are several instances of their concentration to form cemeteries. In the bend of the Boyne, near Slane, are the three great mounds, Newgrange, Dowth, and Knowth as well as a number of unexplored mounds (57) and minor tombs; on the Sliabh na Caillighe or Loughcrew Hills near Oldcastle, Co. Meath, there are thirty tombs; at Carrowkeel, Co. Sligo, there are fourteen tombs, and at Carrowmore, near Sligo, there are (or were) about sixty examples. A less dense concentration is provided by the occurrence on the hill-tops south of Dublin of a number of cairns, some of which are known to cover passage-graves. On the Meath-Dublin border there are numerous hill-top mounds. One of these, at Fourknocks, near the Naul, recently excavated, revealed a cruciform passage-grave with abnormally large central chamber (63). Other mounds exist near the coast in this area. Elsewhere the distribution is thin—northwards as far as Antrim (where there is a small group near Fair Head) and southwards to Kilkenny. It must, however, be realized that the known distribution is possibly very incomplete. Passage-graves tend to retain their mounds (of stones or clay or both) more than do other megaliths—partly because of the inaccessible position of so many and also because the mounds were more substantial

Distribution

than those built over other types of tombs. We cannot, therefore, decide how many hill-top cairns cover megalithic burials.
Any unexplored example is a potential passage-grave but may,
on the other hand, cover merely a simple cist-burial.

The siting of passage-graves, mentioned incidentally, is a
marked feature of the majority of them and especially of the
cemetery-groups. Hill-tops, sometimes quite high
Siting mountain-tops, are favourite sites. Even in the Boyne
cemetery, where there are only low hills, the largest
tombs occur on these summits. The rule is not universal. The
undoubted (now destroyed) passage-grave at Rush, Co. Dublin,
was placed on low ground near the sea, as were the probable
examples at Bremore and Gormanston to the north of it.
The Carrowmore group is not a hill-top concentration (though
the finest monuments there occupy the more commanding
positions); it is also different in other respects. In any case, it is
clear that the passage-graves do not (as do the gallery graves)
indicate a settlement pattern since many of their hill-top
positions would have been inhospitable at any period.

Pots of the type known as Food Vessel occur in passage-
graves in several instances. Although this type of pottery
developed while Beaker ware was still fashionable, it
Date occurs in the passage-graves unaccompanied by Beaker
and therefore evidencing a later stage. But, while this
appears to give the main period of use of the passage-graves,
the date of their beginnings is more doubtful. A heavy type of
pottery, with profuse ornament of large impressions made with
the end of a piece of stick or a bone, comes from several of the
sites, among them Carrowkeel, and it has, therefore, been
called 'Carrowkeel ware'. Fragments of the same ware were
found at Fourknocks, and here as well as at Carrowkeel there
are indications that it is earlier than Food Vessel. At Fourknocks
it was found on the primary mound which contained the
passage-grave and over which the Food Vessels had been
deposited with later burials. The material from early excavations at Loughcrew includes pottery similar to Scottish
Neolithic vessels, some Carrowkeel ware, and some sherds that
probably belong to Food Vessel. Notwithstanding these hints
of pre-Food Vessel dating it seems clear that the main period of
the passage-grave is later than that of the gallery graves.

A notable characteristic of the Irish passage-graves is the occurrence on their stones of carved designs. The designs show great variety—spirals, triangles, lozenges, zig-zags, *Passage-* 'sun-symbols' and others. Two of the passage-grave *grave art* cemeteries have this megalithic art in notable degree —Boyne (58, 61, 62) and Loughcrew. Normally, the motifs are packed or incised, but several of the Newgrange stones have been treated so that the designs are in relief. Some examples of passage-grave art are found south of the Boyne—at Fourknocks (64, 65) and at Seefin and Baltinglass, Co. Wicklow, and a stone with design similar to that of the passage-graves comes from Cape Clear Island, Co. Cork. To the north, art occurs on tombs at Knockmany and Sess Kilgreen, Co. Tyrone, which, for this reason, are connected with the passage-graves though their structure is indefinite.

The engravings on the passage-graves are not art in the ordinary present-day sense of the word. They are rather religious symbols which had a sacred meaning for the tomb builders. What that meaning was we have no means of knowing, nor can we do more than guess at the origin of the designs. Some have been plausibly shown to be conventionalized representations of the human form or of the human face. In a few instances, this is easy of acceptance but in many cases the process of conventionalization has gone far. The designs are paralleled in Brittany and the Iberian peninsula—in Brittany on tombs, in Iberia rarely on tombs but frequently stone plaques, bones, and pottery provide more identifiable prototypes. The megalithic art is one of the cultural connexions which link the Irish passage-graves with Iberia where—in Portugal and Southern Spain—there are many tombs of the same type (though not of the cruciform plan). The basin stones found in the side chambers of the Irish tombs (60), evidently intended to hold the cremated remains of the dead, are also paralleled, though not frequently, in Iberia.

The Sligo passage-graves lack ornament—except for a few designs in the Carrowmore area which are only doubtfully regarded as megalithic art. It has been suggested that painted designs were used at Carrowkeel, but there is no evidence for this. Perhaps the limestone of the tombs was not found to be a suitable medium for carving or perhaps the absence of art indicates a different tradition. It must, however, be noted that the art at Fourknocks is seen on sandstones and slates only. Many of the large structural stones are of limestone, but their condition shows that the original surfaces have decomposed to a considerable depth so that if they were originally ornamented the designs would have disappeared.

Something must be said here of markings found on natural rocks and on large stones forming no part of megalithic tombs.

Rock scribings   Such rock scribings are usually made by pocking, but some (a small sub-group) are incised. Rock scribings are most frequent in the south-west, especially in west Cork and in Kerry (66), but they occur sporadically elsewhere and similar markings are known in Scotland and Northern England, in some cases on the coverstones of cist graves. The designs show some similarities to those on the passage-graves but are in the main of a different type. They consist of cup-marks, cup-and-circle patterns, concentric circles with radial lines, rectilinear markings and other motifs. This group of Irish rock scribings has been named 'Galician Art' because of its similarity to the rock art of Galicia in north-western Spain. As Galicia and South-West Ireland are both copper-producing areas it is thought that the art may have been introduced to Ireland by prehistoric copper miners from north-west Spain.

The Carrowmore tombs (67) though classed with the passage-graves are very different from the elaborate corbelled structures

Carrowmore tombs   elsewhere. They are built simply of uprights and a large capstone but are, or were, surrounded by a circular stone kerb, have vestigial passages made of two or more uprights and are grouped in a cemetery—features that connect them with the passage-graves. It is usual, therefore, to think of them as dolmens which are the result of the degeneration of the corbelled passage-grave (Fig. 5). But the material from Carrowmore includes fragments of Carrowkeel ware and it would not be safe to conclude that these tombs are chronologically at the end of the passage-grave series. They may in large part be the result of local geology. The big glacial blocks used were easily available in the locality and gave a tomb which had none of the difficult building technique of the corbelled structures on the hills at Carrowkeel to the south.

Another group of tombs is characterized by a long narrow passage which widens slightly at the inner end to provide the equivalent of a chamber. The cairn is surrounded by a circular kerb. The absence of clear distinction between the passage and chamber, the emphasis on the passage and the V-shaped plan (the broad end of the V being at the inside) are features which have given varying names to these tombs; 'undifferentiated passage-graves', 'entrance graves', 'V-shaped passage-graves'. Because five of these tombs occur in a small area in east Waterford they are referred to as 'the Tramore group'. Similar structures are found in the immediate vicinity of the great mounds at New-grange and Knowth. Tombs of the same type are known in Brittany, in the Scilly Isles, and in Cornwall, and the Tramore group is taken to be the result of a small colonizing movement, probably from Brittany. Two examples have been excavated in Co. Waterford. One, at Carriglong (71), yielded Food-Vessel sherds and the other at Harristown had a stone axe-pendant with a cremation in the chamber, but a Food Vessel, urns, and a pygmy cup accompanied secondary burials in the cairn.

V-shaped passage-graves

As has been stated, the use of the word 'dolmen' is now usually restricted to tombs of simple construction—characterized essentially by a varying number of uprights supporting a capstone. But one group of simple tombs—at Carrowmore, Co. Sligo—has been already shown to possess features which connect it with the passage-graves. In this group (so called 'B-dolmens') the chamber tends to be polygonal in outline in contrast with another group ('A-dolmens') which have rectangular or wedge-shaped chambers and are regarded as related to the gallery graves. Dolmens of this latter class frequently possess a pair of large matched uprights which not only help to support the capstone but form portals which emphasize an entrance at one end of the tomb, and hence the name 'portal dolmens' is used for this class of megalith. Portal dolmens are well represented to the east of the country, from Co. Down to Co. Waterford (70), they are found also in south Ulster and in the north-west—in Sligo and Donegal.

Portal dolmens

Though the portal dolmen lacks the more complicated structure or difficult building technique of other megalithic tombs it is frequently highly impressive by reason of its immense capstone (the weight of the capstone of the impressive dolmen at Browne's Hill, Carlow (50), has been estimated at 100 tons).

Method of building   The method of raising the capstone is a usual source of speculation and wonder. It was probably achieved by gradually levering it up and propping it on stones or timber until the desired height was reached and then the capstone could be lowered or slipped down on the uprights. A quarryman of the present day can raise and move a large stone in remarkably skilful fashion with nothing more elaborate than an iron bar as a lever and doubtless prehistoric man was equally adept with a long piece of hardwood.

The portal dolmen is sometimes reduced to the very simple form having only three uprights—as at Legananny, Co. Down (68)—but even in these 'tripod dolmens' two of the uprights are matched to form portals (44). In the more elaborate (or better-preserved) specimens the portals flank a slab which closes or partially closes the entrance (69). Because this feature occurs in gallery graves of the northern type and because of the wedge-shaped outline of the chamber in many portal dolmens, these tombs have been regarded as derivative from the gallery class (Fig. 4). But this conclusion is not definite in view of the lack of dating evidence for the portal dolmens. Furthermore their occurrence outside this country (e.g. in southern Britain) gives the problem a wider basis and suggests that the dolmen was possibly introduced as a developed phenomenon.

The selection of hill-top sites by the passage-grave builders and the preference for upland positions and light soils of the gallery-grave people finds no parallel in the siting of the *Siting* portal dolmens, which are frequently on low-lying ground or even in valleys—as is the fine example at Brennanstown, Co. Dublin. The availability of suitable building material—especially a great glacial erratic to provide the capstone without the necessity of long transport could have exercized an influence on the siting of individual tombs.

The custom of erecting dolmen-like structures may have lasted long after the main period of the megalithic tombs. One of the burials in Ring Fort 5 at Cush, Co. Limerick (mentioned above under 'Forts') was covered by a large boulder supported on small stones, and similar 'boulder-dolmens'

have been noted in various parts of the country. The occurrence of boulder-dolmens at the centre of some stone circles will be remarked on when dealing with these *'Boulder-* monuments. Intimately connected with the megali-
dolmens' thic cult are 'multiple-cist cairns' in which the central chamber is sometimes of dolmen form; these will be dealt with below under 'Burial Mounds'.

The more usual burial rite in Irish megaliths was cremation, though inhumed burials have also been found in most of the tomb types, usually side-by-side with cremated re-
Burial mains. The cremated remains sometimes represent
rite many individuals, but some court cairns and gallery graves contained remains of only very few persons. Cremation seems normally to have been performed outside the tomb, but a cremation flue connected with the megalithic structure was found in one case (Doey's Cairn, Co. Antrim); it has parallels in Yorkshire long barrows.

The beginnings of the custom of building chambered tombs coincided with the introduction of the new way of life which is called 'food-producing'—the first great advance
Introduction of in human history. This economic change
food-producing meant that man, instead of precariously depending on the gifts of nature as they could be availed of by 'food-collecting', began to keep domestic animals and to grow crops. These advances began in the Near and Middle East where they were soon followed by the discovery of a knowledge of metal, but in the spread westward the practice of farming outdistanced the practice of metallurgy and so we find in Europe a Neolithic period which is contemporary with the Bronze Age of the more developed East; the same discrepancy occurs between different parts of Europe. The Neolithic Culture was brought to Ireland by different bands of people and from different sources, but in part it was due to the earliest megalithic colonization—about four thousand years ago. So also working of metals must have been forwarded by other megalithic colonists, and we think of the builders of the great passage-graves not only as farmers but also as people who benefited from the exploitation of Irish mineral resources—though the actual exploitation may not have been in their hands.

BURIAL MOUNDS

In dealing with megalithic tombs mention has been made of the mounds of earth or stone which cover or which once covered them. Not all burial mounds, however, contain chambered tombs, and in this section it is proposed to deal with mounds covering other classes of graves and, incidentally, with other burial types.

A burial mound (chambered or unchambered) is usually referred to in this country as a *tumulus* if built of earth and as a *cairn* (or *càrn*) if it is of stone. Usage is not constant, however, and we sometimes find the word *tumulus* used to cover both classes of mounds, while the term *barrow* (used generally in Britain) is applied to the earthen mound. It must be noted, however, that surface appearance gives only limited indications of the material of a mound; a cairn over which a layer of vegetation has grown, may look like an earthen mound or the material may be alternate layers of clay and stone heaped up at the original building of the monument or in part piled on to cover later burials inserted near the surface of the primary mound.

Tumuli, cairns, barrows

Again, it is not always possible to say with certainty if an unexcavated burial mound covers a megalithic chamber or not. In some cases signs of collapse indicate the position of the chamber; the hill-top position of a cairn or its proximity to a group of passage-grave tombs provide *a priori* reasons for believing it to cover a tomb of this type. A great cairn like that at Knocknarea, near Sligo (about 200 feet in diameter) would be presumed to cover a passage-grave because it is situated in a passage-grave area and is placed on a summit. But all the numerous hill-top cairns which are so conspicuous throughout the country do not contain megalithic tombs. Among the smaller cairns and earthen tumuli, many are certainly unchambered and the graves they cover are varied in type and period.

Chambered and unchambered mounds

The burials under burial mounds are sometimes not protected

by any structure, their only covering being the material of the mound itself; they are frequently contained in a cist, normally

Cists   a box-like structure of stone slabs in which an inhumed or a cremated burial is placed. These cists may be either short (i.e. approximately square about 2 or 3 feet across) (76) or long (about 2 feet by 6 feet) (75) and unless grave goods are found with the burial it is not possible to date them, but in general the short cists belong to the Bronze Age, while the majority of the long cists date from after the end of the Bronze Age into Early Christian times, with, fairly certainly, a numerically smaller group which belongs to a much earlier phase—some as early as the Neolithic.

Long cists were, as their shape suggests, intended to contain inhumed extended burials, but cremations also occur in them. When an inhumed burial is found in a short cist the skeleton is usually in a crouched position—placed on one side with the knees drawn up towards the chin (74). In Ireland many crouched burials are accompanied by Food Vessels (though, of course Food Vessels are not confined to this type of burial); in England they are accompanied by Beakers. At any rate we can see these cists as representing a 'single-grave' tradition opposed to the collective burials of the megalithic tombs—though the finding of Food Vessel and Beaker in the megaliths shows that their makers accepted the collective rite.

Not all the cist graves are neat constructions of regular slabs; some are built of large and irregular stones and show similarity

*Multiple-   to the megalithic structures and have perhaps
cist cairns*   relationship to the same tradition (73). At Linkardstown, Co. Carlow, a low mound covered a polygonal cist containing Neolithic pottery; the cist was made of large stones and was almost megalithic in character. A combination of the traditions of megalithic tomb and of single grave is responsible for the type of burial mound known as a multiple-cist cairn. In these the central grave is frequently a dolmen-like structure, while other burials are arranged around it—in cists or unprotected—the whole contained in a cairn which is often comparatively low in height. The central structure of one of these cairns, of which everything else has been removed, remains at Knockmaree, Phoenix Park, Dublin,

and is a small dolmen-type grave. A tomb of more truly megalithic character is that contained in Cairn A at Aghnaskeagh, Co. Louth. Peculiar features are exemplified in some of the multiple-cist cairns—as the star-shaped cairn at Doohatty, Co. Fermanagh, or the asymmetrical arrangement of graves at Mount Stewart, Co. Down.

The megalithic tradition incorporated in the multiple-cist cairns is consistent with an early origin and grave goods of Early or Middle Bronze Age date go to confirm this. Some, however, survived later—that at Knockast, Co. Westmeath, which covered forty-four burials and had no principal central cist, is dated to Late Bronze Age times. Influence from the continental urnfields has been postulated to account for the large number of burials in some of the cairns, but this is hardly tenable in view of their early origins. The sanctity conferred on a site by burial would, in any case, lead to its continued use for subsequent burials; this concentration of graves is not a new phenomenon—it is parallel to the collective burial tradition of the megalith builders. The new feature is the use of separate graves instead of the chamber of the collective tomb.

The kerb which surrounds chambered cairns is found also in many cases around the unchambered type. Near the centre of the cairn at Curraghbinny, Co. Cork, was found *Kerbs and* another setting of stones, smaller than those of the *stone arcs* kerb and arranged in the form of an arc. This feature has been found in a less definite form elsewhere in Ireland and it occurs in Yorkshire and Scotland. It is probably related to the setting of timber posts found in burial mounds in the Netherlands and to the grander counterpart in Stonehenge—the central horseshoe arrangement of stones—and evidently had a ritual significance. One unusually shaped cairn has been mentioned—the star-shaped example at Doohatty, Co. Fermanagh. A cairn at Dun Ruadh, Co. Tyrone was surrounded by a fosse and bank and contains a ring of upright stones with dry walling between. The centre of the cairn appears to have been open; thus giving what is known as a ring cairn, found also in Scotland and repeated at Kealkil, Co. Cork, where a small ring cairn near a stone circle covered a ring of standing stones.

One class of cairn continued to be built until recent times, and the custom still prevails in places, but the cairns are not for burials. They are memorials in commemoration *Recently built* of an event such as a violent death, and are due *cairns* to the practice of each passer-by throwing a few stones on a pile at the site of the happening commemorated. The same custom is followed at certain cairns which form 'stations' on a *turas* where 'rounds' are made in honour of a saint, as at Glencolumbkille, Co. Donegal.

It must, of course, be realized that not all prehistoric burials are covered by cairns or tumuli. Many are found in flat graves which, having no surface indications, are usually *Flat* discovered by accident—as a result of ploughing, *graves* quarrying or such activities. Graves found in this manner are of every possible variety—long and short cists, containing inhumed or cremated remains, earth burials without the protection of a cist, urn burials protected or otherwise. Grave goods with the burial will provide the best indication of date. When these are not present the type of grave gives some indication of its period. A crouched earth burial would with probability be regarded as of Bronze Age date, but an extended burial without other indications of date must remain very uncertain as to its period. The grave goods found with burials in Ireland are scarcely ever of intrinsic value—as are those rich deposits with the dead in say, Egypt, Mesopotamia and other areas. Here they usually consist of pottery vessels, small bronzes—knives or razors—stone implements or ornaments (beads or pendants), or bone ornaments. The pottery vessels are used either to accompany the remains of the dead or to contain the cremated bones. When they accompany the dead it may be accepted that they were placed in the grave as containers of food offerings to help the departed on the journey to the next life.

A tumulus (77, 79) is similar to a cairn except that the material of which it is constructed is earth and not stones. It is usual to find around a tumulus a fosse from which the material of the mound was taken by the builders (80), but some tumuli are built of material—earth or sods—transported from elsewhere and not taken from a surrounding fosse. The fosse may not be recognizable before excavation because it has become filled

59   NEWGRANGE: ROOF OF CHAMBER SHOWING CORBEL TECHNIQUE

E

60   NEWGRANGE: SIDE-CHAMBER SHOWING BASIN STONE

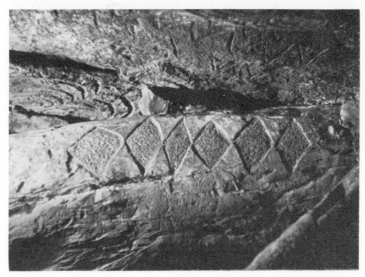

61 NEWGRANGE: DECORATED CORBEL AND PORTION OF ROOFING-
STONE OF SIDE-CHAMBER

62 NEWGRANGE: TRIPLE SPIRAL

63   PASSAGE-GRAVE AT FOURKNOCKS, CO. MEATH, SHOWING CENTRAL
CHAMBER AND PASSAGE

64 FOURKNOCKS: DECORATED LINTEL

65 FOURKNOCKS:
DECORATED UP-
RIGHT IN CENTRAL
CHAMBER

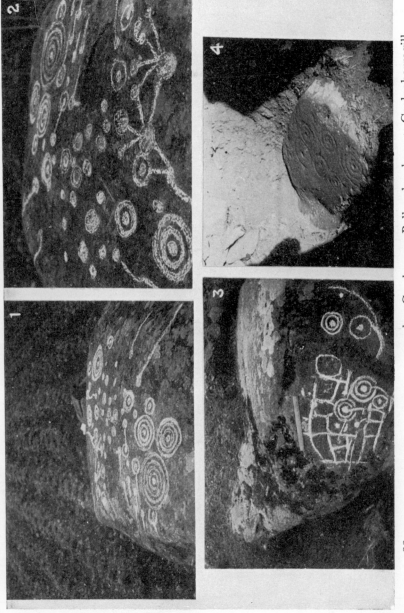

66 ROCK SCRIBINGS, CO. KERRY 1 and 2: Gortboy; 3: Ballynahowbeg; 4: Coolnaharragill

67 "B-DOLMEN", CARROWMORE, CO. SLIGO

68 TRIPOD DOLMEN, LEGANANNY, CO. DOWN

69   PORTAL DOLMEN, HAROLDSTOWN, CO. CARLOW

70   PORTAL DOLMEN, BALLYNAGEERAGH, CO. WATERFORD

71   V-SHAPED PASSAGE-GRAVE, CARRIGLONG, CO. WATERFORD

72   STONE ALIGNMENT, "FINN MACCOOL'S FINGERS", SHANTEMON,
CO. CAVAN

73 MEGALITHIC CIST FROM CHAPELIZOD, CO. DUBLIN
(now in Zoological Gardens, Dublin)

74 CIST BURIAL, KEENOGE, CO. MEATH, SHOWING SKELETON AND FOOD
VESSEL

75   LONG CIST GRAVE AT CUSH, CO. LIMERICK—BROKEN FOOD VESSEL IN
POSITION

76   SHORT CIST GRAVE AT CUSH—URN IN POSITION

77 "MOUND OF THE HOSTAGES", TARA, CO. MEATH

78 BARROW AT RATHJORDAN, CO. LIMERICK

79　TUMULUS AT LATTIN, CO. TIPPERARY

80　TUMULUS AT CUSH, CO. LIMERICK—DURING EXCAVATION, SHOWING
FOSSE

81 STANDING STONE, PUNCHES-
TOWN, CO. KILDARE

82 OGHAM STONE, MINARD,
CO. KERRY

83 STONE WITH IRON AGE
ORNAMENT, TUROE, CO. GALWAY

85 CROSS-INSCRIBED OGHAM STONE,
DROMKEARE, CO. KERRY

84 INSCRIBED STANDING STONE,
BALLYVOURNEY, CO. CORK

86 STONE CIRCLES, GRANGE, LOUGH GUR, CO. LIMERICK

87   STONE CIRCLE, DROMBEG, CO. CORK

88   LISIVIGEEN STONE CIRCLE, KILLARNEY, CO. KERRY

with soil that has silted into it. A mound at Drimnagh, Co. Dublin was built in stages. The primary burial was in a stone cist and was accompanied by an unusual type of pottery bowl; over it a mound of sods and timbers had been built and then burned—aided by an elaborate system of pits and flues to provide draught for the fire.

When the fosse immediately surrounds the base of the mound or when there is no fosse we have the simplest form of tumulus—known in Britain as a *bowl-barrow*, because *Barrow* of its resemblance to an upturned bowl. Where a flat *types* space exists between the fosse and the mound the type is known as a *bell-barrow*. Several other varieties of barrow, known to British archaeology (particularly in Wessex where they have been well studied), have not been recognized here, but one form which consists of a low mound (12 to 30 feet in diameter) surrounded by a ditch and outer bank may be equated with the *saucer-barrow* or when the mound is very slight or non-existent is better referred to under the name *ring-barrow*. (This is the equivalent of the terms used in the Netherlands—*Kringrep*—and in Germany—*Kreisgrab*.)

These ring-barrows are well known in the flat areas of Co. Limerick and some have been noted elsewhere. Frequently they are barely perceptible, having been flattened due *Ring-* to ploughing and other causes. In other cases the *barrows* mound, ditch-and-bank may be well marked. Pottery of Neolithic type has come from some of these monuments at Rathjordan, Co. Limerick (78), Early Bronze Age sherds from others at the same place and one at Lissard, Co. Limerick, produced the remains of an urn (Middle or Late Bronze Age) inverted over cremated bones. Of the many examples of these barrows excavated in Limerick, only this one at Lissard produced any evidence of burial—in others there was presumably an inhumed body so lightly covered that it disappeared without leaving any trace.

Burials dated to Early Iron Age times have been found in larger barrows of this type excavated at Carbury Hill, Co. Kildare. The ritual enclosures on the Curragh, Co. Kildare, are essentially enlarged specimens of ring-barrows—one produced an extended burial but the burial was probably dedicatory. There is no clear dividing line between large

F

ring-barrow and earth-circle ritual site. At Lugg, Co. Dublin, a site enclosed by bank and (outer) fosse was used successively as ritual and burial place.

Low burial mounds have been excavated at Carrowjames, Co. Mayo, and were shown to belong to two groups—one Late Bronze Age, the other Early Iron Age in date.

Not all the interments under burial mounds are contained in formal graves. Under one of the Cush, Co. Limerick, tumuli *Burials* was merely a scatter of cremated bones on the old *without* ground surface where the cremation pyre had been *formal* lighted, and over which the mound had been built. *graves* Under a second tumulus at the same site the cremated bones had been collected into a hole in the old ground surface and with them had been placed a small bone plaque (also showing signs of burning) on which was Early Iron Age ornament. Almost every form of burial has been found in unchambered burial mounds, and their dating, as we have seen, ranges over the whole prehistoric period, but they will often be found referred to in the archaeological literature as a Bronze Age type—in contradistinction to the chambered mounds thus implicitly ascribed to the Neolithic—an over-simplification for both classes.

STANDING STONES

The simplest type of monument with which we deal is the standing stone, which, as it name implies, is merely a stone set upright in the ground. The standing stone is variously *Purpose* known to archaeology as a *monolith* or *menhir* and in Irish as *gallán, dallán,* or *liagán.* Not only is the standing stone a simple form of monument, but also the idea underlying its erection is such a simple one that its simplicity warns us against ascribing it to any one period or cultural context.

The erection of a modern gravestone is essentially similar to the erection of an ancient standing stone, and indeed serves the same purpose as did some of those. Excavation has revealed that standing stones in some cases mark ancient burials. The tall standing stone at Punchestown, Co. Kildare (81), which fell some years ago and was re-erected was found to have at its foot a small cist grave. Again, at the centre of the 'Longstone Rath' (an enclosure, presumably sacred in character, previously mentioned under 'Forts') a standing stone stood beside a long cist grave. Both graves are Bronze Age in type and the finds from the Longstone Rath indicate a date in the Early Bronze Age.

But not all examples were erected to mark burials. It has been concluded that some served as boundary marks, while others marked the line of ancient roadways as in the case of a series of standing stones near Lough Gur, Co. Limerick. It is also thought that some were raised to mark the sites of notable events.

It is clear that certain standing stones were invested with a sacred character as is shown by their presence on ancient ceremonial sites such as the inauguration place at Magh Adhair, Co. Clare and at Tara. Confirmation of this is given by the popular appellation *fear bréagach* sometimes applied to standing stones. Certain highly ornamented stones of Early Iron Age date (with what is known as La Tène ornament carved on them) as at Turoe, Co. Galway (83), were undoubtedly cult objects. So also are holed standing stones with some of which superstitious practices are said to have been associated; these stones are simple uprights perforated with a hole a few inches in diameter.

Other standing stones carry inscriptions in ogham characters or Early Christian crosses or dedications. One cannot, of course, conclude that these inscriptions are always

Inscribed as old as the time of the erection of the stone; some of
standing them may have been inscribed at a later date, but in
stones other cases the stones were certainly erected specifically to bear the inscriptions. The standing stone at Kilnasaggart, Co. Armagh, has on it crosses, crosses-in-circles and an inscription. The inscription gives evidence to date the memorial to about the beginning of the eighth century—a late date for the erection of so crude a memorial.

This span of dating evidence—from Bronze Age burials to Early Christian inscriptions—shows that standing stones in Ireland cannot be ascribed to any one period. Presumably the impetus to their erection in the first instance came with the megalithic culture, which brought the custom of building the great stone tombs, but the date of any single example can only be decided from the evidence it yields to examination (for inscriptions or associations of the site) or excavation. It is likely that even excavation would, in many cases, leave unsolved the question of date.

The custom of erecting standing stones has an important sequel. In early Christian times standing stones began to have crosses and other designs inscribed on them (84, 85); on later slabs the extraneous material is cut away so that crosses of stone are formed and ultimately these give place to the more elaborate ringed crosses with splendid ornament which are among the remarkable achievements of Irish art. It is important to note that the erection of stone crosses is a speciality of Ireland and Britain and must owe much in origin to the prehistoric cult of the standing stone.

Since ogham-inscribed stones have been mentioned above, it may be well to say a few words regarding this form of writing.

Ogham letters are represented by lines up to five in
Ogham number written above, below, or across a stem line.
stones On a standing stone one or more of the corners is usually utilized as a stem line (82). The inscriptions are commemorative, i.e. the name of a person commemorated is given, followed frequently by the name of an ancestor. The language used is Irish, in an early form, and the inscriptions

date mainly from the early centuries of Christianity in Ireland. The majority of the ogham inscriptions come from Kerry, Cork, and Waterford, but others are found through the country as far north as Antrim, and, as a result of Irish influence, in Britain and the Isle of Man. Their interpretation with the aid of the key, which is easily available in the published literature, is perfectly easy if one is dealing with a clear-cut inscription. But, since the inscription has, in almost all cases, become imperfect, through wear or spalling of the stone, its interpretation is best left to an expert who has had long practice. The observant worker may, however, be fortunate enough to discover a hitherto unknown inscribed stone. Such have been found built into farm buildings or used as gate-posts, and as already noted, they are frequently found forming the roofing stones of souterrains.

STONE ALIGNMENTS

Even less can be said of stone alignments than of standing stones. They consist of groups of standing stones arranged in one or more straight lines. They are neither very numerous in Ireland, nor are elaborate forms found here, but they are known elsewhere, as in Brittany and Scotland, where very imposing examples occur. None has been excavated in Ireland and we can only conclude, probably correctly, that stone alignments are monuments connected with prehistoric ritual. A good alignment is found at Castlenalact, near Bandon, Co. Cork, while another occurs at Beenalaght, north of Donoughmore in the same county. The example known as 'Finn MacCool's Fingers' is impressively sited on a hill about three miles north-east of Cavan town (72). Alignments are fairly frequent in the north of Ireland where—in Derry and Tyrone—they are often associated with stone circles.

Pairs of standing stones are known in different parts of the country, and in this arrangement they seem to have, in some cases, a special cult significance, but in others they *Pairs of* can be shown to be nothing more than the gate-posts *standing* of an ancient enclosure, which has been cleared *stones* away. An example occurs near Kilfinnane, Co. Limerick, where two standing stones mark the entrance to a destroyed ring-fort, the outline of which may be discerned when the site is looked at from a neighbouring hill-side. Similarly a pair of stones defines the entrance to a cillín at Oughtihery, near Rylane, Co. Cork.

A concentration of almost three hundred standing stones exists in the townlands of Timoney Hills and Cullaun, near Roscrea, Co. Tipperary. Except for one circle of sixteen uprights, they form no sensible plan at present, but it is possible that they did so before the removal of some of them for road-metalling and other purposes.

In relation to standing stones and stone alignments, a word of warning is necessary. Sometimes a single standing stone or an alignment may not have been erected originally as such. It may in fact be the only remaining part of quite a different structure, most of which has been destroyed, such as a megalithic tomb, a stone circle or an ancient field-fence built with upright stones. A further difficulty arises in the matter of standing stones, since it was the custom to erect stones such as these in recent times as scratching posts for cattle. Tradition is frequently a guide in this matter, but in some districts it may be of little help, especially where the words *gallán* or *liagán* are no longer in use. In these instances, the individual example must be considered on its merits, and one is helped by the general appearance of the stone and perhaps by its relation to other antiquities.

Alignments sometimes remains of structure

STONE CIRCLES

While we have not in Ireland any stone circle as imposing as the English examples at Stonehenge and Avebury we have considerable numbers of stone circles which tend to concentrate in certain parts of the country and which are related in origin and in function to those grander and more famous examples of Great Britain. While many of the Irish circles are small, we have also, as we shall see, some big and imposing sites.

The term 'stone circle' suggests at once the class of monument in question. These monuments consist essentially of a circle of stones enclosing an open area, or, possibly, a *Definition* space in which there is a small burial mound or a stone-built grave. It is well to anticipate here the discussion on function and to state that the term 'stone circle' implies a monument primarily dedicated to ritual. Stone circles must be differentiated from monuments presenting to the casual observer a similar appearance but serving a different purpose. A stone fort with partially demolished ramparts may sometimes look like a stone circle, as may also a circular stone hut-site. Even more difficult is the problem presented by the stone kerb of a burial cairn when the cairn itself has been removed (55). In fact, the sites of cairns of which only the kerbs remain were sometimes marked 'circles' on the Ordnance Maps, for instance at Carrowmore, Co. Sligo.

Stone circles in Ireland are of varied forms. Typical of the west Cork area, where they are very common, are circles of free-standing uprights which vary in number from *Co. Cork* five to fifteen while the diameter of the circle ranges from 10 to about 30 feet. A feature of these circles is the incorporation in them of a so-called 'recumbent stone', a slab set in the ground on its side instead of on end, and having an upper, straight horizontal edge. Diametrically *Recumbent* opposite the recumbent is a pair of matched stones *circles* usually higher than the other uprights. A good example is the circle at Drombeg, near Glandore, Co. Cork (87). A surprising fact regarding the occurrence of the recumbent in Co. Cork is that the only other area in which it is known is Aberdeen where it is found in stone circles of a different type. These Aberdeen circles have a greater number of stones, they enclose a burial cairn and the pair of portal stones flanks the recumbent instead of being on the opposite side of the circle. Four stones placed radially outside the circle at Gowlane North, near Donoughmore, Co. Cork, form an entrance; again they are opposite the recumbent. The Co. Cork circles do not enclose a burial cairn; a ring cairn (with hollow centre) was found immediately beside a small recumbent circle at Kealkil, near Bantry, and excavation showed that the cairn covered a circle of small standing stones, placed concentrically with its circumference. The Kealkil circle exemplifies another characteristic feature of the circles of this area—the possession of an outlier, a large upright stone standing outside the circle. Actually, there are two outliers at Kealkil, though this is unusual. The same feature occurs at Lisivigeen, near Killarney, where a circle of small diameter with six uprights is surrounded by a bank outside which stand two outliers (88).

Instead of a ring of standing stones a stone circle is sometimes composed of a ring of boulders and it sometimes has at the *Circles of* centre a boulder supported on comparatively small *boulders* stones. This feature has already been mentioned in connexion with megalithic tombs as it is clearly a reminiscence of the dolmen type of structure in a very developed form.

Another centre of concentration of stone circles is Co. Tyrone and the neighbouring areas of Fermanagh and Derry. *Co. Tyrone* These circles are usually composed of smaller *circles* stones than those in the Co. Cork ones, but the number of stones is greater. The normal diameter is somewhat less than 50 feet. The largest of the stones are usually only a few feet in height while the majority may be quite low—about one foot high—or may even be small boulders. Many of these stone circles have stone alignments associated with them; these are usually placed tangentially (or approximately so) to the circle. Associated with some of the circles are groups of three standing stones not placed in any constant relationship. The Tyrone stone circles are found on upland areas, above the 500-foot contour, and they are frequently covered (completely or partially) by a growth of peat, their existence, in some cases, being unsuspected until revealed by turf-cutting.

The most remarkable stone-circle site in Co. Tyrone is that at Beaghmore, north-west of Cookstown. The remains here were only very incompletely appreciated before the turf was removed in the course of excavation. It is now known that they extend over several acres and the area already uncovered has revealed a complex system of circles, small cairns, and alignments. One of the circles contains a close setting of small uprights resembling, in appearance, though on a very diminutive scale, the *chevaux de frise* of the Aran forts.

Stone circles of various types occur in the neighbourhood of Lough Gur, Co. Limerick, and these include some of the most remarkable in the country. The most striking and the *Lough* best known of the Lough Gur examples is the great *Gur* circle (in Grange townland) on the western side of the lake (86). This is defined by a contiguous (i.e. placed edge to edge) ring of standing stones about 150 feet in diameter. Outside these is a bank which gives the uprights support and which is 30 feet in width and rises to a height of 4 feet against the stones. Some of the stones forming the circle are immense, the largest being a great upright, rectangular (4 feet by 7 feet) in cross-section, and 14 feet in total height, over 5 feet being sunk in the ground. Nor was the erection of the stones and the piling up of the great bank the total work of the ancient builders; they also covered the whole interior of the circle with clay to a depth of as much as 2 feet so as to hide the unsightly packing-stones placed at the base of the uprights and to provide a level space within. The entrance through the bank was lined at either side with small uprights and gave access to the interior between two large portal stones. The excavation of this site gave important results to which reference will be made below in connexion with the discussion on date.

Another circle on the eastern side of the lake (in Lough Gur townland) is almost as large as the one described; it has a great bank with upright stones at either side of it and at the centre a ring of stones concentric with the outer ones. Excavation showed that a fosse (now silted up) existed inside the bank and that the material for the bank had been taken from the fosse.

Of a different type are those of the Lough Gur circles

composed of a ring of separately placed boulders instead of upright stones. One of these (in Grange townland) has a low mound within it, a similar neighbouring site has no mound nor has the large example at Ballynamona some miles south-east of Lough Gur.

The localities mentioned, though they include the main centres of concentration of stone circles, do not by any means cover the total distribution of stone circles in Ireland. *Other* A number occur in the Kildare-Wicklow border area, *circles* and these include some very fine examples character-ized by stones of considerable size. At Athgreany, near Hollywood, Co. Wicklow, is a circle with outlier at a considerable distance from it, and at Broadleas, Co. Kildare, is a large circle on a low hill-summit. At Kilgowan, Co. Kildare, the small circle of uprights is enclosed by a bank, outside which is a level space surrounded by a bank and fosse. The circle at Ballyfolan, Co. Wicklow, contains a cairn which is hollow at the centre, perhaps due to disturbance, but it is possibly a ring-cairn as at Kealkil.

Stone circles are known in Co. Louth. In Co. Down there is a fine example at Ballynoe which encloses a burial cairn as does also the splendid circle on a hill-top at Beltany, near Lifford, Co. Donegal. A remarkable site at Masonbrook, Co. Galway, consists of a bank with seven standing stones set on it. Excavation did not yield evidence of date.

Close to the well-known stone with Iron Age design at Killycluggin, Co. Cavan, is a stone circle but there is no indication as to its relationship to the carved stone. In the same neighbourhood in Kilnavert townland are small circles of boulders on the summits of hillocks which are surrounded at a lower level by banks, partly stone-faced. These small circles possibly contain burials—some stones at the centre of one site seem to indicate a grave. A similar site on the summit of a conical sand-hill at Whitepark Bay, Co. Antrim, is said to have formerly enclosed a cairn.

The custom of surrounding a burial mound with a circle of stones is shown in its most impressive form at Newgrange where twelve great standing stones remain out of a probable total of thirty-four, placed approximately concentric with the kerb of the cairn (56). A similar feature on a smaller scale appears elsewhere. Another mound at Newgrange about half a mile east of the great passage-grave is surrounded by a *Circles around mounds* circle of stones which is not a kerb since it is separated from the mound proper by an annular space only slightly higher than the surrounding ground. A megalithic tomb at Castledamph, Co. Tyrone, is surrounded by a stone circle. Again a low mound in Ballyanny townland near Nenagh appears to have a kerb and also a concentric ring of stones outside it. This phenomenon of a ring of stones encircling a burial mound is of interest in relation to the origin of the stone circle, but before dealing with this matter consideration must be given to the question of the date of stone circles in Ireland.

Stone circles are notoriously disappointing in the matter of datable finds. No evidence of date was obtained in several excavated sites—the large stone circle east of Lough Gur, the Kealkil site, the similar one at Muisire Beag, Co. Cork and one at Castledamph, Co. Tyrone. The extensive site at Beaghmore yielded a stone axe and a few sherds of unidentifiable pottery; that at Ballynoe, Co. Down, gave one sherd which was provisionally declared to be Neolithic.

Fortunately, however, abundant material came from one site—the great stone circle in Grange townland, west of Lough *Date* Gur. A considerable amount of pottery was found, mainly in the neighbourhood of the uprights where it had, perhaps, been broken ritually, as seems to have occurred on some of the Brittany stone circles. On the Lough Gur site there were also flints, stone axes, bone points, and some bronze. The pottery included Beaker, among which was a vessel (an 'A-Beaker') that closely resembled one discovered in Somerset as well as other ('B') types similar to those found on the Lough Gur habitation sites. With the Beaker were other classes of pottery, notably examples of well-developed Food Vessel. The material gives a date in the Early Bronze Age, say about the eighteenth century B.C. and the different types of pottery suggest that different groups of people co-operated in the construction of the monument. Excavation showed that this circle had not been used for habitation and had no burials —negative evidence which indicates its having been built for ritual purposes.

The dating—to Beaker times—of one example does not imply that all Irish stone circles are of this date. It does agree with the main body of evidence for the stone-circle *Origin* cult in Britain, though there the story is extended back to earlier times by the argument that certain circles belong to very early in the Beaker period or even to the Neolithic. These early circles are the so-called 'henge' class. This term is derived from Stonehenge and from its wooden counterpart, discovered by aerial photography, for which the name 'Woodhenge' was coined. Strictly speaking the word 'henge' is applicable to monuments with lintels on the up-rights—a feature for which Stonehenge alone presents evidence —but the term is, by extension, used to cover all sites with free-standing circular settings of posts or stones surrounded by ditch-and-bank or even those with ditch-and-bank only. Stone circles without enclosing ditch-and-bank and also those with stones set in the bank are, in Britain, regarded as a separate class.

The pottery from the henges shows similarity to ware known in the Netherlands where there occur burial mounds in which the burial is surrounded by a palisade of upright posts set in the mound—probably representing a house or perhaps actually built as a house around the grave. It is argued that this is the origin from which the henge monument develops and the further suggestion has also been made that some of the British henges were roofed temples.

While the Dutch palisade mound may provide something of the origin, two other considerations are important. In the first place a palisaded burial mound is not a henge, and the creation of this type complete with ditch-and-bank is an insular development. Secondly, the megalithic contribution must have been of essential importance. In fact it is only by recognizing something of the mixed origins and the complex development that we are able to appreciate the diversity of expression of the ritual idea as seen in the stone circle and related monuments.

The megalithic contribution to the origin of the stone circle can readily be acknowledged in view of what we have learned of the structure of megalithic tombs. We have seen that New-grange and other Irish burial mounds were surrounded by a circle of stones, as was also Kercado in Brittany, evidently to delimit a sacred area around the tomb. More striking in this context is the forecourt—usually semicircular, sometimes circular as at Los Millares—which is found before the *Dual* entrance to many Iberian passage-graves. We know *tradition* also that the court cairns have semicircular or circular areas marked by standing stones, and that similar ritual courts are associated with the tombs and temples of the west Mediterranean, in Sardinia and Malta. This dual tradition, on the one hand of a stone-defined ritual enclosure connected with tombs and, on the other, of circular wooden houses, not only indicates the mixed ancestry of the ritual circle but also helps to account for the variety of its forms. The megalithic ritual enclosure was used by the living as the centre in which they would perform their funeral or other religious rites; it was connected with the dead by these rites and by its structural association with the tombs. Similarly the house, primarily a habitation for the living, readily became a tomb for the dead or a temple for worship. Hence we find the stone circle sometimes associated with burials, sometimes without any such association. Some remain, as they began, ritual enclosures around burials, though the burials, no longer under magnificent tombs as at Newgrange, may be covered by meagre cairns or contained in small cist graves and may be merely dedicatory in purpose. Others have no burials; they are purely ritual sites and in certain instances special features (outlier and recumbent) emphasize their purpose. Even if we stress the ritual purpose of stone circles, we are far from being able to say in what that ritual consisted. Circles were presumably places of assembly for the population groups to whom they belonged and such assemblies were, doubtless, occasions of ceremonial and conclave. For parallels to these ceremonials we might invoke the practices of modern primitive peoples whose dances take place around structures similar to our circles but the comparison, valid probably on broad lines, is not likely to help in the matter of detail.

The use of stone circles as observatories or as centres of sun-worship has frequently been discussed and we must allow for such a purpose in the case of certain examples, especially those that have outliers and recumbent stones. Further evidence of the use of some circles in this manner is adduced from their orientation (the alignment of the main axis towards the rising or setting sun on a particular day of the year). There is no doubt that orientation was considered important by prehistoric man not only in stone circles but in some megalithic tombs; its importance has been obscured by the extravagant claims made by its protagonists who have sometimes argued about orientation as if primitive man used modern precision instruments.

Orientation

Some indication has been given of the structural variety of Irish stone circles. In general it is clear that the essential idea was the provision of an enclosed space for ritual and this general concept links to the stone circles the monuments which are defined by ditch-and-bank without stone structure. Certain examples—of stone circles and of earth circles—qualify as henges under the British definition of the term, but in Ireland there is no geographical distinction between the distribution of henge and non-henge types (as is claimed for Britain), and the available data are too meagre to allow of differentiation in the matter of date and cultural affinities. It is clear that the ritual earthen enclosure began early and lasted to the end of prehistoric times. At Rathjordan, Co. Limerick, an oval area defined by a low bank outside a ditch was built in Beaker times—contemporary with some of the small ring-barrows from which it could have developed, and also with the quite different site, the Grange stone circle. Other embanked ritual enclosures have been enumerated when we dealt with forts. It appears likely that stone circles and earth circles influenced one another so that mixed forms resulted. We have no clear evidence of an Irish stone circle being built or used as late as Iron Age times, though such late dating is attested elsewhere; late Iron Age pottery found at Stonehenge shows that there were structural additions made there shortly before the Roman invasion. There is the well-known story of St. Patrick destroying the idols at Magh Slecht, but this has been shown to be a medieval invention to account for the features of a known stone circle and is therefore of no value as an early testimony.

Earth circles

On the other hand, ritual circles of earth were used at a late date. The ditch-and-bank enclosures on the Curragh, Co. Kildare, were almost certainly Iron Age in date and the Curragh is known from historical references to have been an ancient assembly place. Other assembly and inauguration places also have ritual earthworks and the case which has been *Late* made for the functioning of a Druidic priesthood *survival* at Stonehenge could also be made for these sacred places of Celtic Ireland in the centuries immediately preceding the introduction of Christianity. As Stonehenge has its very early beginnings and a late survival of sanctity, the Irish sites also are a development of types which originate equally early.

SUGGESTIONS FOR FURTHER READING

ABBREVIATIONS OF NAMES OF PERIODICALS

A.N.L.   The Archaeological News Letter (London)
Ant. J.   The Antiquaries Journal (London)
Arch. Jour.   The Archaeological Journal (London)
C.L.A.J.   County Louth Archaeological Journal
I.N.J.   Irish Naturalists' Journal
J.C.H.A.S.   Journal of the Cork Historical and Archaeological Society
J.G.A.H.S.   Journal of Galway Archaeological and Historical Society
J.R.S.A.I.   Journal of the Royal Society of Antiquaries of Ireland
N.M.A.J.   North Munster Antiquarian Journal
P.P.S.   Proceedings of the Prehistoric Society
P.R.I.A.   Proceedings of the Royal Irish Academy
T.R.I.A.   Transactions of the Royal Irish Academy
U.J.A.   Ulster Journal of Archaeology

GENERAL WORKS

Macalister, *Ireland in Pre-Celtic Times*, Dublin and London, 1921, and *The Archaeology of Ireland*, London, 1928. This latter is the most useful general text-book. It is unfortunately out of print, but may be obtained in almost any library. The value of the later (1949) edition is less because of theoretical considerations not generally accepted. Raftery, *Prehistoric Ireland*, London, 1951, has numerous illustrations but lacks a bibliography. Wood-Martin, *Pagan Ireland*, London, 1895; out of date but useful because well illustrated and gives classified lists of published papers on different types of antiquities, as does also the same author's *Traces of the Elder Faiths of Ireland*, 2 vols., London, 1902. Mahr, 'New Aspects and Problems in Irish Prehistory', *P.P.S.*, 3 (1937), 261; particularly valuable as a summary of work and discoveries during the decade prior to publication. The work of the period from 1937 to the end of World War II is summarized in Ó Ríordáin, 'Prehistory in Ireland, 1937–46', *P.P.S.*, 12 (1946), 142. Northern Ireland is dealt with by Davies in *U.J.A.*, 11 (1948) to 12 (1949).

Short but comprehensive accounts of Irish Archaeology will be found in the *Saorstát Eireann Official Handbook*, Dublin, 1932, in the *Encyclopaedia Britannica* and in *Encyclopedia Americana*.

Childe, *Prehistoric Communities of the British Isles*, London and Edinburgh, 1940, treats Irish prehistory as part of the general development in Great Britain and Ireland, and provides an excellent account which fully covers work up to 1939. Later editions (1949) contain inserted passages dealing with subsequent research. Brief accounts of British prehistory of value to the Irish student are Clark, *Prehistoric England*, London, 1940; J. Hawkes and C. Hawkes, *Prehistoric Britain*, in Pelican Books, 1943, and an extended version, London, 1947; Piggott, *British Prehistory*, London, 1949. For the general European development see Hawkes, *The Prehistoric Foundations of Europe*, London, 1940; Childe, *Prehistoric Migrations in Europe*, Oslo, 1950.

A Preliminary Survey of the Ancient Monuments of Northern Ireland, Belfast, 1940, lists, and in many cases illustrates, the more important monuments of the Six-County area. The introductory chapters give general accounts of megaliths, forts, souterrains, and other types. See also the small illustrated booklets: *The National Monuments of the Irish Free State*, Dublin, 1936; *Ancient Monuments of Northern Ireland in State Charge*, Belfast, 1928; *Ancient Monuments of Northern Ireland not in State Charge*, Belfast, 1952. Brief accounts of Irish monuments will be found in *The Provinces of Ireland* series (edited George Fletcher), Cambridge, 1921 and 1922.

FIELD-WORK AND SURVEYING OF ANTIQUITIES

Field Archaeology: Some Notes for Beginners, issued by the Ordnance Survey, London, 1932. This little booklet, though issued specially for Britain, will be found most helpful by Irish workers. Selected bibliographies are given for each type of monument. Williams-Freeman, *Field Archaeology as Illustrated by Hampshire*, London, 1915, provides examples of how to survey. Atkinson, *Field Archaeology*, London, 1946; a useful introduction to field-work. The beginner in field archaeology will be well advised to consult some published papers dealing with the survey of a definite area, e.g. Price, 'The Ages of Stone and Bronze in Co. Wicklow', *P.R.I.A.*, 42 (1934), 31; Hartnett, 'The Megalithic Tombs of East Muskerry', *J.C.H.A.S.*, 45 (1940), 71; O'Kelly, 'A Survey of the Antiquities in the Barony of Small County, Co. Limerick', *N.M.A.J.*, 3 (1942), 75 to 4 (1944), 222. For surveys of earthworks some of the papers of Knox and Westropp in *J.R.S.A.I.* and *P.R.I.A.* might be consulted. An article by Leask, 'The Archaeological Survey', *J.R.S.A.I.*, 72 (1942), 1, gives particulars of methods of map location and filing, the adoption of which by all workers would tend to uniformity of recording. Interesting descriptive notes (unfortunately not illustrated) of the antiquities of Millstreet district will be found in Timothy Broker, *Sraid an Mhuilinn, A history of its people by its people for its people*, Millstreet, 1937.

Those interested in local history study apart from archaeology might profitably read: Pender, 'How to Study Local History', *J.C.H.A.S.*, 46 (1941), 110; Gleeson, 'Sources for Local History in the Period 1200–1700', *ibid.*, 46 (1941), 123. For place-names see Price, 'The need for a Study of Irish Place Names', *N.M.A.J.*, 1 (1936), 29; and for folklore: Ó Súilleabháin, *Láimh-Leabhar Béaloideasa*, Baile Átha Cliath, 1937 and Ó Súilleabháin, *A Handbook of Irish Folklore*, Dublin, 1942.

FORTS

Westropp, 'The Ancient Forts of Ireland', *T.R.I.A.*, 31 (1896–1901), 579. This is the most comprehensive account of Irish forts, and gives adequately the state of knowledge regarding them at the beginning of this century. Numerous other papers by the same author deal with forts of special areas and with headland forts of the whole coast. References to them and to other relevant publications will be found in Macalister, *Archaeology of Ireland*. (In general in this bibliography earlier papers are not included and for references to them the reader is directed to Macalister and Wood-Martin. Therefore, in this and the following sections only more recent papers and earlier ones of some especial interest will be included.)

RESULTS OF EXCAVATIONS. Macalister and Praeger, 'Report on the Excavation of Uisneach', *P.R.I.A.*, 38 (1928–9), 69 and 'The Excavation of an Ancient Structure on the townlands of Togherstown, Co. Westmeath', *ibid.*, 39 (1930–1), 54; O'Neill Hencken, 'Cahercommaun: A Stone Fort in County Clare', *R.S.A.I.*, Extra Volume, 1938; Ó Ríordáin, 'Excavations at Cush, Co. Limerick, 1934 and 1935', *P.R.I.A.*, 45 (1940), 83 and 'Excavation of a Large Earthen Ring-Fort at Garranes, Co. Cork', *ibid.*, 47 (1942), 77; Childe, 'A Promontory Fort on the Antrim Coast', *Ant. J.*, 16 (1936), 179; 'Doonmore, A Castle Mound near Fair Head, Co. Antrim', *U.J.A.*, 1 (1938), 122; Davies, 'Excavations at Lissachiggel', *C.L.A.J.*, 9 (1939), 209; 'Corliss Fort Excavation', *C.L.A.J.*, 9 (1940), 338; Ó Ríordáin and Foy, 'The Excavation of Leacanabuaile Stone Fort near Caherciveen, Co. Kerry', *J.C.H.A.S.*, 46 (1941), 85; Macalister, 'The Excavation of Kiltera, Co. Waterford', *P.R.I.A.*, 43 (1936–7), 1; Ó Ríordáin and Hartnett, 'The Excavation of Ballycatteen Fort, Co. Cork', *P.R.I.A.*, 49 (1943), 1; O'Kelly, 'Excavation of a ring-fort at Garryduff, Co. Cork', (Preliminary Report) *Antiquity*, 20 (1946), 122; Ó Ríordáin, 'Lough Gur Excavations: Carraig Aille and the Spectacles', *P.R.I.A.*, 52 (1949), 39; Ó Ríordáin and MacDermott, 'Excavation

of a Ring-Fort at Letterkeen, Co. Mayo', *P.R.I.A.*, 54 (1952), 89;
Evans, 'Rath and Souterrain at Shaneen Park, Belfast, Townland
of Ballyaghagan, Co. Antrim', *U.J.A.*, 13 (1950), 6; O'Kelly, 'An
Early Bronze Age Ring-Fort at Carrigillihy, Co. Cork', *J.C.H.A.S.*,
56 (1951), 69 and 'Three Promontory Forts in Co. Cork', *P.R.I.A.*,
55 (1952), 25.

For the theory of over-all roofing of ring-forts see Bersu, 'Three
Celtic Homesteads in the Isle of Man', *Journal Manx Museum*,
5 (1945–6), 177, and *ibid.*, 'The Rath in Townland Lissue, Co.
Antrim', *U.J.A.*, 10 (1947), 30. See also Ó Ríordáin, 'Three
Marshland Habitation Sites', *J.R.S.A.I.*, 79 (1949), 138; the literary
evidence is given briefly in *A.N.L.*, January 1952, p. 73.

DISTRIBUTION OF FORTS. Evans and Gaffikin, 'Megaliths and Raths',
I.N.J., 5 (1935), 1; Watson, 'Prehistoric Sites in South Antrim',
U.J.A., 3 (1940), 142; Davies, 'Types of Rath in Southern Ulster',
U.J.A., 10 (1947), 1.

HILL FORTS. Orpen, 'Rathgall, Co. Wicklow', *J.R.S.A.I.*,
41 (1911), 138 and in *P.R.I.A.*, 32 (1913), 41. On a Neolithic
hill-top camp, see Evans, 'Lyles Hill: A Prehistoric Site in Co.
Antrim', *City of Belfast Museum and Art Gallery Quarterly Notes*,
64 (1940), 1. For short report on excavation at Freestone Hill, see
Bersu in *Old Kilkenny Review*, No. 4 (1951), 5.

MOATED HOUSES. O'Neil, 'A Square Fort at Ballyraine, near
Arklow', *J.R.S.A.I.*, 71 (1941), 26.

ANCIENT FIELDS, ROADS, and LINEAR EARTHWORKS. Knox, 'Some
Connacht Raths and Motes', *J.R.S.A.I.*, 41 (1911), 301, and other
papers in *ibid.*, 44 (1914), 45 (1915), 48 (1918); Davies 'Ancient
Field Systems and the date of the formation of the peat', *U.J.A.*,
2 (1939), 61; Power, ' "The Rian Bó Phádruig" (The Ancient High-
way of the Decies)', *J.R.S.A.I.*, 35 (1905), 110; Lawlor, 'An Ancient
Route—The Slighe Miodhluachra in Ulaidh', *U.J.A.*, 1 (1938) 3;
Ó Lochlainn, 'Roadways in Ancient Ireland', *Féil-Sgríbhinn Eoin
Mhic Néill*, Dublin, 1940, p. 465. For the Black Pig's Dyke and the
Dorsey see Kane, *P.R.I.A.*, 27 (1908–9), 301, and *ibid.*, 33 (1916–17),
539; Tempest, *C.L.A.J.*, 7 (1930), 187; Davies, *U.J.A.*, 3 (1940), 31;
C.L.A.J., 9 (1938), 131 and *ibid.*, 9 (1940), 280.

MOTTES. Leask, *Irish Castles*, Dundalk, 1941. For references to
earlier controversy see Macalister, *Archaeology of Ireland*, p. 354. See

reference to Doonmore under 'Results of Excavations' above. See also Lyons, 'Kilfeakle and Knockgraffon Motes, Co. Tipperary', *J.R.S.A.I.*, 80 (1950), 263.

CILLÍNÍ. Ó Súilleabháin, 'Adhlacadh Leanbhai', *J.R.S.A.I.*, 69 (1939), 143; Power, 'Ballygarran Cill, near Waterford', *J.R.S.A.I.*, 71 (1941), 64; Henry, *Irish Art*, London, 1940, p. 24. On hill-top churches see Davies 'Church Architecture in Ulster', *U.J.A.*, 6 (1943), 61. For a discussion of *Cillíní* see Power, 'The *Cill* or *Cillín*: A Study in Early Irish Ecclesiology', *Irish Ecclesiastical Record*, 73 (1950), 218.

SOUTERRAINS

Many of the references to forts, as given above, will be found of interest also in relation to souterrains. For numerous references see Macalister, *Archaeology of Ireland*; Wood-Martin, *Pagan Ireland*. Scottish souterrains: Childe, *Prehistory of Scotland*, London, 1935. Cornish souterrains and discussion of distribution: Hencken, *The Archaeology of Cornwall*, London, 1932. A list of many Co. Cork souterrains is given by Gogan, *J.C.A.H.S.*, 34 (1929), 1. Discussion of date of souterrain building: Mongey, 'Souterrain at Millerstown, Parish of Stradbally, Co. Waterford', *J.R.S.A.I.*, 69 (1939), 162.

HOUSE-SITES

Macalister, 'On an Ancient Settlement in the South-West of the Barony of Corkaguiney, Co. Kerry', *P.R.I.A.*, 31 (1896–1901), 209. 'Conditions of Life in Prehistoric Ireland', *U.J.A.*, 3 (1940), 5 (compiled by members of the Editorial Board)—a useful brief summary of various aspects of prehistoric life in Ireland. Ó Ríordáin and Hunt, 'Mediaeval Dwellings at Caherguillamore, Co. Limerick', *J.R.S.A.I.*, 72 (1942), 37; Davies, 'The Twomile Stone, a Pre-historic Community in Co. Donegal', *ibid.*, 72 (1942), 98. The house-sites excavated at Lough Gur are not yet fully published but a summary is to be found in *P.P.S.*, 12 (1946), 147; see also Ó Ríordáin and Ó Danachair, 'Lough Gur Excavations: Site J, Knockadoon', *J.R.S.A.I.*, 77 (1947), 39. Henry, 'Habitation Sites on Inishkea North, Co. Mayo', *J.R.S.A.I.*, 81 (1951), 75; O'Kelly, 'St. Gobnet's House, Ballyvourney, Co. Cork', *J.C.H.A.S.*, 57 (1952), 18. For French clocháns see Henry, 'Early Irish Mon-asteries, Boat-shaped Oratories and Beehive Huts', *C.L.A.J.*, 11 (1948), 296.

COASTAL DWELLING SITES

Hewson, 'Notes on Irish Sandhills', *J.R.S.A.I.*, 65 (1935), 231; *ibid.*, 66 (1936), 154; *ibid.*, 68 (1938), 69; Evans, 'A Sandhill Site in Co. Donegal', *U.J.A.*, 4 (1941), 71; Raftery, 'New Early Iron Age Finds from Kerry', *J.C.H.A.S.*, 45 (1940), 55; Ó Ríordáin, 'Recent Acquisitions from Co. Donegal in the National Museum', *P.R.I.A.*, 42 (1935), 145; Brunicardi, 'The Shore-Dwellers of Ancient Ireland', *J.R.S.A.I.*, 44 (1914), 185; Coleman, 'The Kitchen Middens of Cork Harbour', *J.C.H.A.S.*, 43 (1938), 39.

ANCIENT COOKING-PLACES

Wood-Martin, *Pagan Ireland* for references. Ó Ríordáin, 'Fulacht Fiadh: Discovery at Kilnagleary, Co. Cork', *J.C.H.A.S.*, 42 (1937), 57; Broker, *Sráid an Mhuilinn*, 10; for description of wooden trough near Mallow see *J.C.H.A.S.*, 2 (1893), 262. Description of a site in Warwickshire with discussion on the method of use, in *Trans. of the Birmingham Archaeological Society*, 1927, 291. For Wexford examples see Ranson, *J.R.S.A.I.*, 75 (1945), 54.

CRANNÓGS

Wood-Martin, *The Lake Dwellings of Ireland*, London, 1886; Davies, 'Trial Excavation at Lough Enagh', *U.J.A.*, 4 (1941), 88; Raftery, 'Knocknalappa Crannóg, Co. Clare', *N.M.A.J.*, 3 (1942), 53; Hencken, 'Ballinderry Crannóg No. 1', *P.R.I.A.*, 43 (1936), 103; and 'Ballinderry Crannóg No. 2', *ibid.*, 47 (1942), 1; Davies, 'Contributions to the study of Crannógs in South Ulster', *U.J.A.*, 5 (1942), 14. Ó Ríordáin and Lucas, 'Excavation of a small Crannóg at Rathjordan, Co. Limerick', *N.M.A.J.*, 5 (1946–7), 68; Hencken, 'Lagore Crannóg', *P.R.I.A.*, 53 (1950), 1; Davies, *Excavations at Island Mac Hugh*, Belfast, 1950.

Added in press: Numerous sites have been discovered at Lough Gara (Sligo–Roscommon border) as a result of the drainage of the lake: *J.R.S.A.I.*, 82 (1952), 182.

OTHER STRUCTURES IN BOGS. Macalister, 'An Ancient Road in the Bog of Allen', *J.R.S.A.I.*, 62 (1932), 137; Mitchell and Ó Ríordáin, 'Early Bronze Age Pottery from Rockbarton Bog, Co. Limerick', *P.R.I.A.*, 48 (1942), 255; O'Toole, 'Ancient Structures recently found in bogs', *J.R.S.A.I.*, 73 (1943), 25; Price, 'St. Broghan's Road, Clonsast', *J.R.S.A.I.*, 75 (1945), 56.

MEGALITHIC TOMBS

Borlase, *Dolmens of Ireland*, 3 vols., London, 1897; an old work which is still extremely valuable. Wood-Martin, *The Rude Stone Monuments of Ireland*, Dublin, 1888; the examples are largely drawn from Co. Sligo.

No attempt is made here to give a list of articles dealing with the excavation of individual sites, and the following papers are mentioned because they contain general discussion of some aspect of megalithic tombs: Evans, 'Giants' Graves', *U.J.A.*, 1 (1938), 7; Powell, 'The Passage Graves of Ireland', *P.P.S.*, 4 (1938), 239; 'Megalithic Tombs in South-Eastern Ireland', *J.R.S.A.I.*, 71 (1941), 9 and 'A New Passage Grave Group in South-Eastern Ireland', *P.P.S.*, 7 (1941), 142; Daniel, 'The Dual Nature of the Megalithic Colonization of Prehistoric Europe', *P.P.S.*, 7 (1941), 1; Mongey, 'The Portal Dolmens of South-Eastern Ireland', *Journ. Waterford Spelaeological Soc.*, 1 (1941), 1; Davies and Evans, 'The Horned Cairns of Ulster', *U.J.A.*, 6 (1943), 7; de Valera in Ó Ríordáin, *P.P.S.*, 12 (1946), 150; Piggott and Powell, 'Notes on Megalithic Tombs in Sligo and Achill', *J.R.S.A.I.*, 77 (1947), 136 and discussion of this paper in de Valera and Ó Nualláin, 'The Megalithic Tombs of the Island of Achill', *J.R.S.A.I.*, 80 (1950), 199; Daniel and Powell, 'The Distribution and Date of the Passage Graves of the British Isles', *P.P.S.*, 15 (1949), 169; de Valera, 'A Group of "Horned Cairns" near Ballycastle, Co. Mayo', *J.R.S.A.I.*, 81 (1951), 161. On Megalithic art and rock scribings see MacWhite, 'A New View on Irish Bronze Age Rock Scribings', *J.R.S.A.I.*, 76 (1946), 59.

BURIAL MOUNDS

For general classification and typology of barrows, see Grinsell, 'The Bronze Age Round Barrows of Wessex', *P.P.S.*, 7 (1941), 73.

Results of recent excavations: Kilbride-Jones, 'The Excavation of a Composite Tumulus at Drimnagh, Co. Dublin', *J.R.S.A.I.*, 69 (1939), 190; Willmot, 'Three Burial Sites at Carbury, Co. Kildare', *J.R.S.A.I.*, 68 (1938) 130 and 'Two Bronze Age Burials at Carrowbeg North, Co., Galway', *J.G.A.H.S.*, 18 (1939), 121; Hencken, 'A Cairn at Poulawack, Co. Clare', *J.R.S.A.I.*, 65 (1935), 191 and 'A Tumulus at Carrowlisdooaun, Co. Mayo', *ibid.*, 65 (1935), 75; Hencken and Movius, 'The Cemetery-Cairn at Knockast', *P.R.I.A.*, 41 (1934), 232; Riley, 'Excavations in the Townland of Pollacorragune, Tuam, Co. Galway', *J.G.A.H.S.*, 17 (1936), 44; Raftery, 'The Tumulus Cemetery of Carrowjames,

Co. Mayo', *J.G.A.H.S.*, 18 (1939), 157 and *ibid.*, 19 (1940), 16; Ó Ríordáin, 'Excavation of a Cairn in Townland of Curraghbinny', *J.C.H.A.S.*, 38 (1933), 80 and 'Excavations at Lissard, Co. Limerick and other sites in the locality', *J.R.S.A.I.*, 66 (1936), 173, also Cush paper cited under 'Forts'. The findings at Lissard are corrected in Ó Ríordáin, 'Excavation of a Barrow at Rathjordan, Co. Limerick', *J.C.H.A.S.*, 52 (1947), 1; *ibid.*, 'Further Barrows at Rathjordan Co. Limerick', *J.C.H.A.S.*, 53 (1948), 19; MacDermott, 'Two Barrows at Ballingoola', *J.R.S.A.I.*, 79 (1949), 139; *ibid.*, 'Excavation of a barrow in Cahercorney, Co. Limerick', *J.C.H.A.S.*, 54 (1949), 101, Kilbride-Jones, 'The Excavation of a Composite Early Iron Age Monument with "Henge" Features at Lugg, Co. Dublin', *P.R.I.A.*, 53 (1950), 311; Ó Ríordáin, 'Excavation of some Earthworks on the Curragh, Co. Kildare', *P.R.I.A.*, 53 (1950), 249; O'Kelly, 'Excavation of a Cairn at Moneen, Co. Cork', *P.R.I.A.*, 54 (1952), 121—Moneen is an example of a multiple-cist cairn; see also Letterkeen, listed under 'Forts' above.

STANDING STONES

Leask, 'The Long Stone, Punchestown, Co. Kildare', *J.R.S.A.I.*, 67 (1937), 250; Macalister, Armstrong and Praeger, 'A bronze-age interment with associated standing-stone and earthen-ring, near Naas, Co. Kildare', *P.R.I.A.*, 30 (1912–13), 351; O'Toole and Mitchell, 'Grooved Standing Stones in Carlow and Kildare', *J.R.S.A.I.*, 69 (1939), 99 and Mitchell, *ibid.*, 70 (1940), 164.

OGHAM STONES. Macalister, *Studies in Irish Epigraphy*, I, London, 1897, II, ditto, 1902, III, ditto, 1907; Power, *The Ogham Stones, University College, Cork*, Cork, 1932; Macalister, *Corpus Inscriptionum Insularum Celticarum*, vol. I, Dublin, 1945.

STONE ALIGNMENTS

Ó Ríordáin, on alignment at Castlenalact in *J.C.H.A.S.*, 36 (1931), 63; Mahr, on Roscrea concentration in *P.P.S.*, 3 (1937), 363; For alignments associated with Stone Circles see Davies, *U.J.A.*, 2 (1939), 2.

STONE CIRCLES

For a general discussion of Stone Circles see Kendrick, *The Druids*, London, 1927, Chap. v; Hawkes, *Prehistoric Foundations of Europe* (numerous references). For Irish examples see Somerville, 'Five Stone Circles of West Cork', *J.C.H.A.S.*, 35 (1930), 70 (pays a great deal of attention to orientation); Davies, 'Stone Circles in Northern

Ireland', *U.J.A.*, 2 (1939), 2; 'Excavations at Clogherny', *ibid.*, 2 (1939), 36; 'Castledamph Stone Circle', *J.R.S.A.I.*, 68 (1938), 106; Gogan, 'A Small Stone Circle at Muisire Beag', *J.C.H.A.S.*, 36 (1931), 9; Ó Ríordáin, 'Excavation of Stone Circle and Cairn at Kealkil, Co. Cork', *J.C.H.A.S.*, 44 (1939), 46. The Magh Slécht Legend: Duignan, *Féil-Scríbhinn Eoin Mhic Néill*, Dublin, 1940, p. 296. Suggested reconstruction of timber circles: Piggott, 'Timber Circles, a re-examination', *Arch. Journ.*, 96 (1940), 193. Lough Gur circles are described by Windle, 'Megalithic Remains immediately surrounding Lough Gur, Co. Limerick', *P.R.I.A.*, 30 (1912), 283. The excavation of the largest is dealt with in Ó Ríordáin, 'Lough Gur Excavations: The Great Stone Circle (B) in Grange Townland', *P.R.I.A.*, 54 (1951), 37. For discussion of henge monuments see Atkinson, Piggott, and Sandars, *Excavations at Dorchester, Oxon*, Oxford, 1951.

For earth circles see references above under 'Burial Mounds' to Rathjordan and to the Curragh and under 'Standing Stones' to '. . . earthen ring near Naas'.

INDEX OF PLACES

The index includes places in Ireland only. Spelling normally follows that used by the Ordnance Survey but in some cases a variant spelling which has been given general currency in archaeological literature is retained. References to photographic illustrations are in round brackets; the numbers of pages on which line drawings are to be found are given in square brackets. Grid reference to the map is given by letter and number (e.g. N15).

University Paperbacks

A COMPLETE LIST OF TITLES

Titles marked thus: * are to be published during 1966

ARCHAEOLOGY AND ANTHROPOLOGY

ART AND ARCHITECTURE

BIOGRAPHY

ECONOMICS

LAW

LITERATURE

SCIENCE